Praise for *In the Black* and **T. Dallas Smith**

"My friend Dallas has written an uplifting book about his journey in the field of commercial real estate. He describes his humble start to the top of the tenant representation field in Atlanta. His portrayal of being Black and young while overcoming prejudice and hurdles is delivered, not with bitterness, but with calm determination to succeed. This book is a worthwhile read."

—ANDREW L. GHERTNER
Vice Chairman, Cushman Wakefield of Georgia, Inc.

"I met Dallas when he was nineteen years old. Upon coming to the office for an interview, it was obvious to me he was anxious to get his 'foot in the door' and learn all he could about real estate. Dallas was like a sponge, spending as much time as possible with Mr. Tift, soaking up all the knowledge he could. He had an outgoing personality, which is definitely an asset in real estate. He just seemed to climb the ladder with his determination and faith. It was not always easy, but he continued on regardless of the obstacle.

I've worked for Mr. Tift for over forty years. Looking back and remembering the time Dallas started work with us, and watching as he grew and prospered, just does my heart good. I am so proud of him. And his book *In the Black* is a must-read for anyone of any color, race, creed, or gender. It proves that you can do it if you work hard enough."

—SUSAN CHRISTY
Former President, Atlanta Air Center Realty

"T. Dallas Smith is a champion for change who continues to inspire and influence others. *In the Black* takes you on his personal journey through walls of adversity, heartache, and unrelenting perseverance. Dallas's story is transformational!"

—JOHN F. O'NEILL III
President, US Multifamily Capital Markets, Cushman & Wakefield

"This book tells you: Dallas is the super underdog who can see the stars in the daytime. He instigates hope, amplifies confidence, redefines the meaning of *dream* to dream big for all those underdogs to awaken."

—YOUNG WOO
Founder and Principal of Young Woo and Associates, LLC

"*In the Black* is definitely a MUST-READ! T. Dallas Smith has a great sense of humor and a good-hearted way of telling his real story. I both laughed and winced uncontrollably as I relived with him the everyday experience of a Black man in a white Atlanta world and felt it viscerally. It was a real eye-opener for me … No, a soul-opener!"

—W. ALLEN MORRIS
Chairman and CEO, The Allen Morris Company, and author of ALL IN: How to Risk Everything for Everything that Matters

"In his book, *In the Black*, my friend and colleague T. Dallas Smith masterfully uses his life journey to both learn and teach. His success in life is the result of his unwavering commitment to excellence and his willingness to engage people to find common ground. He makes the compelling case that personal relationships are the foundation of an enduring society."

—EGBERT L. J. PERRY
CEO, Integral Group, LLC

"Dallas tells his remarkable life story in a very intimate, inspiring, and transparent way. There are life lessons for everyone in this book. I was particularly struck by his enduring decision to choose optimism over bitterness. As a Black man in a predominantly white man's industry, he faced challenges I have never known. Yet he has conducted himself with elegance and purpose throughout his career. The courage and leadership he has consistently demonstrated continue to make real and long-lasting impacts on the commercial real estate industry. They were long overdue. We are better for it because of Dallas."

—STEVE DILS
Managing Director and Principal, Avison Young

"Dallas Smith, with his combination of drive, openness, and resilience, mixed with a wicked sense of humor, has described a path to success not only for Black real estate professionals, but all professionals. I am proud to call him friend and member of my 'personal board of directors'."

—MITCHELL E. RUDIN
Chairman and Chief Executive Officer, Savills USA

IN THE BLACK

T. DALLAS SMITH

IN THE BLACK

CHANGING THE DOMINANT NARRATIVE IN THE COMMERCIAL REAL ESTATE INDUSTRY

Forbes | Books

Published by Forbes Books, Charleston, South Carolina.
Member of Advantage Media.

Forbes Books is a registered trademark, and the Forbes Books colophon is a trademark of Forbes Media, LLC.

Printed in the United States of America.

10 9 8 7 6 5 4 3 2 1

ISBN: 978-1-95588-459-4 (Hardcover)
ISBN: 978-1-95588-460-0 (eBook)

LCCN: 2022918994

Cover design by David Taylor.
Layout design by Analisa Smith.

Since 1917, Forbes has remained steadfast in its mission to serve as the defining voice of entrepreneurial capitalism. Forbes Books, launched in 2016 through a partnership with Advantage Media, furthers that aim by helping business and thought leaders bring their stories, passion, and knowledge to the forefront in custom books. Opinions expressed by Forbes Books authors are their own. To be considered for publication, please visit **books.Forbes.com**.

To everybody who's ever thought about being in commercial real estate and everyone who ever thought they were not enough, couldn't do it, didn't come from the right place, didn't have the right connections, who were told no, that they were too young, too black, too anything. In the Black *is for you.*

CONTENTS

ACKNOWLEDGMENTS

In the Black is dedicated to everybody who's ever thought about being in commercial real estate and everyone who ever thought they were not enough, couldn't do it, didn't come from the right place, didn't have the right connections, who were told no, that they were too young, too black, too anything. *In the Black* is for you. It's my story about how I got into commercial real estate—how I dealt with the good, the bad, and the ugly. But please know that you can do whatever you want and that you are more than enough.

I am reminded of the story when I was selling clothes at J. Riggins at Perimeter Mall in Atlanta, Georgia, in 1982. A woman came in with her husband, and she said, "He has no suits, and he needs everything." He stood there completely silent. I started, "Well, every man should have a blue suit, a gray suit, a black suit, and a brown suit." And I went through the process. I connected each suit with the proper shirts, ties, and socks. Everything I put together she loved. I rang up the sale and it was over $2,000, which was a very big sale for J. Riggins, the biggest sale I'd ever made for the store. She was a well-dressed white woman, and I asked her, "If you don't mind me asking, what do you do for a living?" In a very condescending manner she stated, "I'm in real estate!" I responded, "Oh, I want to be in commercial real estate." And this woman said to me, "You'll never make it! You're Black. And you're too young. You might have a chance in residential, but you'll never make it in commercial." Later that same year, I started in commercial real estate.

I wish I knew who that woman was so I could tell her all the things that have happened in my life since she made that statement. Being named Realtor of the Year by the Atlanta Commercial Board of REALTORS and Broker of the Year by the Empire Board of Realtists, Inc. in 2018, receiving the Alvin B. Cates award in 2020 for the most impactful deal done in the state of Georgia in 2020, doing the largest deal in the United States in 2020 for Microsoft of 523,000 square feet, being named Most Admired CEO by the *Atlanta Business Chronicle* for both 2017 and 2021, and now serving as president of the Atlanta Commercial Board of REALTORS in Atlanta, Georgia, the largest commercial real estate board in the country. I have received many more awards than the ones I named. I don't state these things to brag; I state these things in contrast to the statement that a stranger made to me.

I'm so grateful to my parents, my mother in particular, who always told me you can do and be whatever you want to do. I only tell that story for this simple reason: I hope that this motivates you to think that, if this guy who grew up off Simpson Road in Atlanta, Georgia, in the zip code 30314, who wasn't supposed to make it, has grown the largest African American tenant rep firm in the country from nothing, indeed you can too! Happy reading.

FOREWORD

If you work in the commercial real estate industry or aspire to, this book is a must-read. It will inspire, challenge, motivate, and encourage.

The expression "in the black" is commonly heard in the financial world and refers to a company's most recent financial status, its last accounting period. The phrase has a positive connotation. When a company is in the black, it is said to be profitable, financially solvent, and not overburdened by debt. The team at T. Dallas Smith & Company is "in the black" in many ways. The company is majority African American / Black, which is both positive and unique in commercial real estate. Its founder turned a negative into a positive by overcoming challenges to break into a nondiverse—and *still* nondiverse—industry as well as by reaching back and lifting as he climbs, mentoring, hiring, and inspiring people who look like him to realize their full potential.

My first interaction with T. Dallas Smith & Company was at the annual CoreNet Global Conference in Seattle, Washington, in 2018. I drove over that morning from the east side of the Seattle metropolitan area (Redmond, Washington), the home of Microsoft Corporation, to the Washington State Convention Center. After I registered, I started mingling with the attendees for more than a few minutes when a young gentleman approached me and asked, "Are you Michael Ford?"

"Yes, I am."

"I'm Cedric Matheny from T. Dallas Smith & Company. We have been looking for you."

"Why is that?"

"We wanted to meet the head of Microsoft's real estate organization."

The conversation continued from there, with the rest of the T. Dallas Smith & Company team joining in. Later, we attended a few breakout sessions together and enjoyed a group lunch, after which I invited the team to tour the Microsoft headquarters.

Microsoft is a massive organization that employs over 180,000 employees globally and has a diverse workforce. My career with Microsoft started seventeen years ago in Finance, and my Microsoft career path has given me the opportunity to work in different groups within the company. Approximately six years ago, I became the head of Global Real Estate. I immediately recognized there were only a few minorities in the commercial real estate team at Microsoft and quickly realized there were very few in the industry. I witnessed firsthand the challenges they faced. Diversifying the real estate team was a necessity and one of my top priorities.

Internal to Microsoft, I wanted to drive change by recruiting qualified and skilled employees from diverse cultures and backgrounds. I began personally mentoring employees and pushing them to meet their highest potential. We have also been successful at retaining diverse employees by continuously looking for ways to support and promote those who are eligible.

Externally, I wanted to find minority-owned businesses like T. Dallas Smith & Company to work with and support. I could see that

Dallas and I shared the same goal of making commercial real estate an industry that welcomes diversity. We both believe in reaching back and lifting up those who have been historically excluded from the profession.

T. Dallas Smith & Company is responsible for helping Microsoft procure ninety acres of land in one of Atlanta's predominately African American and distressed neighborhoods. Microsoft is creating spaces for this community to live, work, and play by building affordable housing, creating jobs, and giving residents a place to unwind, recharge, and thrive. Supporting and revitalizing the neighborhood is a historical event for Microsoft and Atlanta. Our community-first approach will allow Microsoft to work with the local government and community to give African Americans a neighborhood they can be proud to call home. As the head of Microsoft's commercial real estate organization, I am proud of the history we are making, and T. Dallas Smith & Company deserves the credit for helping us find a neighborhood we are excited to support.

Microsoft and I understand that our suppliers should represent our diverse consumer base. So long as minorities continue to be underrated and underrepresented, we will continue to make history by supporting and investing in diverse businesses.

I've always believed that diversity is the key that unlocks unlimited possibilities in business. The ideas and skills that employees from diverse cultures and backgrounds bring to the company are invaluable, and policies and habits of inclusion and respect for people with different opinions and beliefs create a dynamic that promotes growth.

Breaking into a nondiverse industry may be challenging, but it is not impossible. T. Dallas Smith & Company is proof that arduous work and fierce determination lead to success. Dallas understands that representation matters, that entry-level employees need to see executives who look like them.

T. Dallas Smith is on a mission to make history by diversifying the faces of the commercial real estate industry, and this book is sure to inspire, challenge, and ignite readers' passion for dreaming and achieving along with him. I know Dallas agrees with me about the importance of thinking big, striving for greatness, and remembering to pave a path for future leaders as you climb the ladder to success. In other words, I think we are in agreement about the value of staying *In the Black*!

Michael Ford

Microsoft CVP of Global Workplace Services

INTRODUCTION

Anyone I've ever known—Black or white—who'd met David Schwartz during their time as a student at Georgia State either loved him or hated him. If you talked to almost anybody Black, you'd hear that Dr. Schwartz was the biggest racist you were ever going to meet. If you talked to any of the white students, you'd hear that Schwartz was the biggest asshole. Only occasionally, you'd talk to a person—Black or white—who'd tell you that David Schwartz had absolutely changed their life for the better.

I've always been the kind of person who needs to see for myself. I'm just hardwired that way. Intrigued by what seemed like a helluva contrast between his haters and his admirers, I'd registered for one of Schwartz's introductory two-hundred-person classes and gotten myself a front-row seat the first night. At the time, I was already working in commercial real estate. That meant I was showing up to evening classes in my work attire: suit and tie, French cuffs, perfectly polished shoes.

If he's horrible, I thought, I'm just going to quit school at the end of the night and focus on my career full time.

Georgia State is the largest school in Georgia, both now and when I attended in the early 1980s. Back then, less than 5 percent of the students at the university were African American, and in this class, as with several others, I was the only Black person.

The classroom was a big theater-style hall with a lectern set up on a platform at the front. As we were all waiting for the professor to arrive, the door swung open to reveal a frail-looking man in a suit and tie smoking a cigarette. He drew a last leisurely puff, then put the cigarette out right on the No Smoking sign. From my front-row seat, I could see all the other divots where I assumed he'd put out hundreds of cigarettes before.

Okay, I thought, this is different.

Schwartz lurched his way toward the podium with a very pronounced, almost Herman Munster–quality limp. He put down his things—briefcase from one hand, loose papers from another—then carefully tucked his cigarettes into his breast pocket as he got up onto the stage. He leaned into the microphone and in a surprisingly raspy voice announced, "My name is David J. Schwartz, and I am the CEO of this class. You, you are all my employees. I will not pay you with money, but I will pay you in grades."

He turned to the two-story chalkboard behind him and pushed one panel to the side. In huge print—you would have had to use a ladder to get up so high—was a list of positions within the classroom "corporation":

One president = A

Ten vice presidents = Bs

Sixty-four managers = Cs

Seventy stock boys = Ds

Fifty-five janitors = Fs

It all added up to a neat two hundred. When Schwartz announced that there would be only one A grade in the class—reserved for the class president—about fifty people picked up their things and walked out.

I was even more intrigued.

Next, Schwartz switched gears. "You heard from me; now let's hear from you." He looked at the audience and pointed at me, so I got out of my seat and walked up onto the stage. Schwartz was still standing behind the lectern and did not move.

"Excuse me," I said politely, but he didn't move. "Excuse me," I tried again. Dude, I thought, you want to hear from me? I need you to be out of my way. I'm going to tell you my story, but I need you to move. Okay?

After the third polite ask, well, I gently moved him to the side myself.

"Hello," I said into the microphone. "My name is Dallas Smith. Currently I'm working for Atlanta Air Center Realty. I was just promoted to marketing director. And I'm in this class to find out more about marketing because I know it's going to change my life."

I don't really remember the rest of what I said, but I do remember that in the middle of me talking, Schwartz started banging on the desk.

"What is your name?"

"Dallas Smith."

"Smith, let me tell you: you have it! Whatever it is, you have it! Twenty years from now, when all of you are at a reunion judging people by the size of their limousines, your limousine is going to stretch longer than this building. You're going to sit on boards. You're going to be an influential advisor ..."

He went on, naming all these things that in my heart of hearts I wanted but had never uttered to another living soul. Here was this white man I'd just met telling a room full of white people my secret desires.

I was hooked.

I became president of the class; ultimately, Schwartz became a trusted mentor and advisor, and later both a client and a friend. He died in 1987 at the age of sixty, and not a day goes by when I don't think about all that I learned from him and from the book he wrote that so influenced my development, *The Magic of Thinking Big*.

I took every class that Schwartz taught and changed my major from real estate to marketing after the day he made the following argument: "You can be a doctor, a lawyer, a whatever, but if nobody knows that you're a doctor or a lawyer, you're going to be a broke doctor, lawyer, or whatever you are. Whatever you do, you've got to be able to sell, sell, sell!"

I came to believe that Schwartz was neither a racist nor an asshole. Instead, he was someone with a strong distaste for people who didn't work hard. It didn't matter if you were Black, white, Asian—if he didn't think you worked hard, you were going to have a hard time with him. That's how he was hardwired.

> There's a commonality I've noticed in the way that billionaires and other extremely successful people talk ... they don't use any limiting words.

Schwartz's lessons mean so much more to me now than they did when I first got to know him in my midtwenties. I'm still realizing the true magic of thinking big—and of speaking big too. There's a commonality I've noticed in the way that billionaires and other extremely successful people talk. The way I'd explain it is this: they don't use any limiting words. They don't say, "No, I can't do this or that," and they don't hesitate. They don't even use tentative words like *try* or *maybe*. Their speech is as big as their ideas; there's absolutely no limit. Exciting possibilities, even risky ones, are met with a hearty "Let's do that!" Jeff Bezos wants to go to the moon? "Okay, let's go to the moon!" Schwartz was essentially giving us all a lesson in getting to the moon, but he also expected us to put in the effort necessary to take the trip.

Being Schwartz's protégé turned me into something of a monster. It made me popular with the other students, and I let that go to my head, forgetting that some of the attention they directed toward me was simply to get on my good side. You see, the class president was the one who got to help Schwartz assign everyone else's grades. That meant there were always a lot of people who wanted to ride with me. I'm pretty sure they figured that if they could be friends with me, they'd at least come out with a B in the class.

By the third of Schwartz's classes, I had amassed a whole group of Dallas fans. When I was late to register for my fourth class with him, I also arrived late to the classroom and peeked through the narrow window before opening the door. I caught sight of the other Black person in the class, Yolanda Anderson, who mouthed to me, "Are you in this class?" When I nodded my head yes, her eyes grew wide, and she put her hand up to her mouth. I looked over at the desk at the front of the room, and instead of seeing Schwartz there, I saw a student I did not know sitting there talking to the group. I knew immediately that he was president of the class.

Okay, that's that, I thought, before opening the classroom door. I'm in my career; I'm making money, so even though I'm trying to sneak into the room, I'm still the only Black man there, and I'm dressed in an Armani suit—white shirt, red tie, to be exact.

Everyone noticed when I entered the classroom, and when Schwartz saw me, I launched into an explanation. "Dr. Schwartz, I apologize for being late. There was a problem, but I'm registered now." I started making my way to the back of the room. "I'll just take that empty seat over there."

That's when Schwartz said, "Hold on, hold on ..." then turned to the class. "How many of you know Smith?" Half the class raised their hands. They knew Smith.

"Half these people don't know you, Smith. Come up here. Go sit down," he told the guy perched up front on the desk, who also didn't know Smith and whose face had turned crimson.

"Class," Schwartz continued, welcoming me to the front of the room, "I want you to meet your new president."

I soaked up every second I could of Schwartz's free time. I'd walk with him to and from class, knowing that just being around him was going to make me feel seven feet tall and bulletproof. A couple of days after that class, we were walking to his office when he handed me a piece of paper, saying, "Look at this!" It was a course withdrawal slip from the guy who had spent some minutes as class president before I'd shown up late. Schwartz followed up with "I knew he didn't have what it takes!"

Schwartz liked big. So I gave him big. People from outside of class would come to see my presentations just to see how I was going to top what I'd done the last time. Newt Gingrich's second wife, Marianne, was in one of my classes, and she planned ahead to make sure that Newt could be there when I presented. After class, Newt approached me with an offer to work with him in DC. If I had any political aspirations at that time, they were vague enough that the desire to remain in Atlanta won out over the invitation to start on a new career path in the nation's capital.

In my final class with Schwartz, everyone was waiting to see how I could possibly top my other presentations. And everyone in class had started copying me, which is to say that they were coming in with bigger and bigger presentations of their own. If I was going *this big*, then they were going to try to go even bigger. I should clarify that the aim in Schwartz's classes wasn't just to emulate the president; it was to try to take the president's job. It was a very competitive environment that he created. In past presentations, I'd brought in props, models, music—everything you could think of. But by that last class, I'd noticed that everyone had started copying me, so I took my final presentation in a completely opposite direction.

The assignment was to present what we were going to do for the rest of our lives.

Schwartz was perched on the very edge of his desk. "Smith, are you ready?" he rasped. "Where's your PowerPoint?"

"I don't have a PowerPoint."

"Where are the models and the live music?"

"I don't have any of that."

"Well, what do you have?"

I took a single piece of chalk out of my jacket pocket, walked up to the board, and wrote my name—T. Dallas Smith—and underneath that, The Dallas Group. I continued to explain the details as I diagrammed a plan for my own commercial real estate firm. I was going to hire ten brokers, and each broker was going to make a half million dollars … and on I went, mapping out the entire project.

Then I turned to my fellow students, whose responsibility it was to punch holes in my vision. I knocked out answers to their questions left and right. When we finished, Schwartz said quietly but with a big smile, "I've never seen any shit like that before."

He was proud. I was proud because he was proud. And that is the story of the first time I shared what I intended to create. Essentially, I mapped out the very work I'm doing today at T. Dallas Smith & Company, though at the time, I didn't know that I would first run away from that calling before committing to go after it with everything I had.

Schwartz's book had made him famous, selling over three million copies in its first years after publication. He'd joined Georgia State as one of the biggest-name professors in the department, but eventually a new guy came to town: Thomas Stanley. Stanley's book, *The Millionaire Next Door*, had also sold big.

I enrolled in one of Stanley's classes, ready to impress him with all I'd learned from following Schwartz. Picture me having taken every Schwartz class, with *The Magic of Thinking Big* as my main reference point, turning out more and more over-the-top final presentations. Then I get into Stanley's class, and my instinct is to do the exact same thing. My first assignment was a case study of a company that made small motors. Naturally, my presentation began with a friend of mine playing the keyboard—the theme song from the hit TV show *Dallas*—as I walked into the room. The keyboard he played used one of the company's motors. Next, models in bikinis passed out virgin piña coladas made with a blender that also used one of the company's motors.

If you've ever read Stanley's book, *The Millionaire Next Door*, you'd know that it could not be more opposite from Schwartz's. If Schwartz was big, big, big, Stanley was all about small, small, small. The typical millionaire, he argued, lived quietly in a $250,000 house, drove a Ford F-150 pickup, and didn't wear fancy suits. And there I was bringing Schwartz to his class. I also brought my entourage of people who'd gotten Bs in the last class they took with me, thinking I could do no wrong. After we finished the presentation, I sat there thinking, Yeah, we killed it; we just killed it!

We got our grades the next class. I earned a C. I was like, What the hell? Of course, I needed to go immediately to Dr. Schwartz's office like I was running to my daddy.

"You won't believe what happened!" I was still reeling as I threw the grade in front of Schwartz. "Look at this!"

"Come on," he said. "Follow me."

Together, we marched down to Tom Stanley's office, Schwartz already gearing up to straighten him out.

"Tom, do you know this man right here?" he inquired, as Stanley continued to read the newspaper stretched out before him at arm's length.

"Yeah." Stanley didn't even look up from the page.

Schwartz handed over the piece of paper. "Smith doesn't get Cs. Smith gets As. And if you and I are going to continue to be friends, you're going to change this grade from a C to an A."

"Well, I guess we won't be friends."

Schwartz and I tucked our tails and walked solemnly back to his office.

"Well, Smith, you're on your own on this one."

On my own, I ended up figuring out two things quickly. First, these were two totally different guys with two totally different takes on success; I couldn't bring a Schwartz presentation to a Stanley class. I'd forgotten that I needed to know my audience. Second, I wanted to learn from Stanley as much as I had from Schwartz.

So I just did that. No more models in bikinis. From then on, I was very Wall Street and stayed focused on the facts. Learning has always been a very tactile process for me, and I tend to learn by imitating, literally becoming like the people or ideas I'm trying on. I had to bring my suits down a notch to make that work, so I went to JCPenney and picked up a regular blue suit, a couple of button-down shirts, and some penny loafers. I knew how to be myself while also being a bit of a chameleon, and I wanted to try on Stanley's point of view—to mirror him in every way, from his ideas down to his style—to see just how that felt.

What each of these two teachers had to give to me, I took in wholeheartedly. Schwartz boosted my confidence in a way that I continue to marvel at and appreciate. Stanley taught me to pay attention to practical concerns. I might have started out focusing on the guys with the gold chains and the Mercedes, but I came to realize that there were people who appeared to be rich and weren't, just as there were people who appeared to be middle class, even poor, but were rich.

Schwartz wanted me to wake up in the morning and make sure that I looked sharp, because if I looked good, I'd feel good and not be afraid in the face of challenges. Stanley wanted me to know that I could wear khaki pants, be humble, and still have confidence and long-term wealth. In mimicking them both, the effect on me was that their views sort of neutralized each other on the one hand, and sort of sat comfortably together on the other. I'm still more Schwartz than Stanley, and probably more Schwartz than most, but I developed an understanding of them both that enabled me to fit them together in a way that made sense to me.

That's probably because even though Stanley was all about data and statistics, he was also, at heart, a mountain mover. For him, whatever got in your way, your job was to figure out how to overcome it. Whether you had to drill through the mountain, climb it, or fly over it—whatever you had to do, the important thing for Stanley was much the same as it was for Schwartz. If you allowed yourself to be stopped by the mountain, that was on you. For both, it was on you to figure out how to make the move that would get you past the mountain.

Both Schwartz and Stanley gave me the confidence and the knowledge I needed to be able to move forward in my career. And now, for the first time in my life, I'm able to be the person who does for others what those two giants did for me. I'm putting my effort into creating an environment within the field of commercial real estate that I wish had existed when I was coming up. I work every day to give young entrepreneurs who look like me the confidence, the knowledge, and the opportunity to move forward and make a name for themselves in this business.

When I wrote out my business plan for that final presentation in Schwartz's class, I was working for Tommy Tift, who had brought me into the commercial real estate business. From there, I moved to Cushman & Wakefield, and after that, I worked for Herman J. Russell and then for Brian Jordan before starting my own firm. It was Mr. Tift—a white man—who gave me my start, but it was Mr. Russell who showed me how to do this work as only a Black man can do it.

What I mean by that is very simple. When you're Black, you're going to have a different experience than white people—I mean that down to the smallest detail, even shopping for groceries or driving a car. We all drive our cars, but me driving a car as a Black man is different. I can't tell you how many times I've been pulled over for driving while Black. I consciously choose to drive a Kia instead of a Mercedes or Porsche or Range Rover or any of those other more obvious luxury vehicles. I used to drive some of those other cars, but experience taught me to do otherwise. I grew tired of cops pulling me over, their first question to me "Is this your car?" And then, as if offering sense-making explanation to this Black man outfitted in his fancy suit with French cuffs, "We've had a lot of cars stolen around here."

I learned a lot from Mr. Russell about how to navigate the world, including the highest levels of power, while being Black. He taught me that there's an art to it. Part of that art goes back to a lesson that Tom Stanley made sure I understood: you don't need to be flashy. What Herman J. Russell added—or reminded me of—is this: there are a lot of situations in which you can't be flashy.

The reality in America is that Black people know white people much better than white people know Black people. That's just a fact. But I say it repeatedly and emphatically to the people who work for me, because they work in a white person's world. It's important for us to remember that the difference between a Black person getting home safely and a white person getting home safely still rests on us knowing how to read and interact with white people. We are always learning what to do and what not to do as we negotiate whiteness. But if you're a white person, you don't have to know anything about us to feel safe in the world.

Don't be mistaken, negotiating whiteness can also give us a leg up. Ray Charles called it being "country dumb." Herman J. Russell did it. Herman J. Russell was a master at it, like James Bond listening to a criminal tell him the entire plan and then just taking the necessary steps to follow through on what he'd learned to defeat his opponent. A lot of white people, because sometimes they don't even see Black people, will just give away the entire plan.

That puts white people at a disadvantage—when they think all we're doing is serving them tea at that dinner or shining their shoes while they talk about their investments or their opinions. One of the wealthiest Black guys I know is a shoeshine man; he's been shining shoes for over thirty-two years and has listened to the conversations of as many CEOs of major companies. Some of them became his friends, but others treated him more like a piece of furniture. He knew how to deal with it when he was treated that way, but that doesn't mean he stopped listening to them making deals and trading stocks and sharing information that they assumed he couldn't benefit from.

I feel comfortable saying that I've been around a lot more white people than most white people have been around Black people. Hell, my industry is still only 3 percent Black. But for all that, and knowing as I do how to negotiate whiteness, I still get frustrated that things haven't changed all that much.

Not that many years ago, I was at one of the more exclusive private clubs in Georgia at an industry leadership event. It was my honor that day to introduce a colleague of mine who was being inaugurated president of the organization. As I approached my seat at the president's table, a white man walked past and stopped me to ask, "Are you out of mimosas?"

"Huh?" I hadn't yet registered why he was asking.

Now, the help at this club was predominantly Black. They had on tuxedos, name tags, the whole uniform. I was in a blue suit, white shirt, and red tie, but all this man saw was Black. I was heated, but like I said, I'd learned how to negotiate moments like these.

We've still got a lot of work ahead of us in this industry. I'm still often the only one who looks like me in rooms full of wealthy white people.

I mention that recent incident to say this: we've still got a lot of work ahead of us in this industry. I'm still often the only one who looks like me in rooms full of wealthy white people. And even given my career success, I still get asked if I'm out of mimosas.

That's part of the reason I firmly believe that what I'm supposed to do with my life from this point forward is make sure that I make a place for people who look like me to succeed in this industry. And part of doing that is sharing with you the story of how I negotiated my own path—not because I think it should be imitated but because I think it's important to share my experiences with those who may need to see that there is, in fact, a history, a lineage of Black commercial real estate success stories to which they might someday add their names.

Here's the last thing I'll say before we get deeper into this narrative: To me, sharing my story requires that I be authentic. And in my opinion, being authentic requires making myself vulnerable. That's what I intend to do here—the same as I've done when making friends and conducting business. It's what I believe I owe to everyone I meet. You'll see from the stories in this book that I put myself out there because I really do believe that the best quality I have to offer is my vulnerability. Really, it's all any of us has to offer if we're trying to be genuine human beings, to really meet people when we're introduced to them, and to build strong and lasting relationships.

Back in the mid-1990s, I participated in a race awareness workshop led by civil rights leader C. T. Vivian. That workshop was life changing for me in many ways, but I distinctly remember one of his lessons in particular: one way that Black people continue to condone racism is by not confronting our friends about their racist views and actions. "In reality," I remember him saying, "you may be the only Black friend they have. And if you don't speak the truth to them, where are they going to get it from?"

That just stuck with me.

I've always thought that when you show somebody who you really are, it's up to them how they handle it. So when I'm vulnerable with the people I meet, and when—as you'll see—I've made friends and family of white people with some surprising histories and profiles, I know it's up to them how they receive me and whether or not they reciprocate my openness. That's also why I haven't been deterred from the belief that I might be able to find the best in people, or from the conviction that it's imperative for me to see for myself who people really are.

I'm telling you my story not just because I want to help people see how a blue-collar Black man from Atlanta found success in a white man's industry that has created more millionaires than basketball, football, and baseball combined. I'm telling you my story because I want to speak the truth, to leave everything on the table—the plans for the building, the keys to the front door—for the generation of Black men and women who come after me, so that their experiences in this profession will be that much better than my own.

CHAPTER 1

The Nose of a King

I was eight years old when I became an entrepreneur. On the day it happened, my mother was washing dishes wearing a muumuu and matching scarf, her hair still in rollers. I'd come into the room to get a snack from the refrigerator, and we started up our usual banter. For whatever reason—maybe because I have two older sisters or because I was born premature—my mom kept me close. We were always around one another, always in easy conversation.

Above the kitchen sink at 200 Childs Drive was a big picture window that looked out onto the neighbor's yard.

"Ty," Mom said, "you should ask the Flanigans if you can cut their grass."

"How much should I charge?" was my first and only question.

"Five dollars."

I bolted out the front door and over to the Flanigans'. I knocked on their door like it was a 911 emergency; they greeted me with looks of intense worry on their faces.

"Ty, what's going on?"

"Hi. Can I … can I … can I cut your grass?" I was out of breath and gulping in air.

Their expressions softened into big smiles. "Sure. So how much are you gonna charge?"

"Five dollars."

"Okay." Mr. Flanigan grabbed a bowl off the table to his right, counted out five silver dollars, and passed them over to me.

I ran back to my mom with bounty in hand, holding it up to make sure she could see all of it. "Look!"

"I guess you got to cut the grass now." She smiled.

The thing was, I couldn't crank the mower. I could pull it out from under the crawl space and bring it around to the front of the house, but that's when I needed an intervention. My mom—still in her muumuu, scarf, and curlers—came down the front steps and cranked it for me.

The Flanigans were very pleased with my work and asked what time I was planning to be back next week. That was the first moment I'd thought about how cutting grass wasn't just a one-off activity. I would have to do it multiple times.

I got a calendar from the kitchen drawer and started marking all the dates that I figured I'd be cutting grass. In my head, I was calculating the number of mows I would need to complete to be able to buy this go-kart I had my eye on. If I could cut the grass every three days, I could have that go-kart in under three months.

Mom saw me working on my calendar and offered some guidance. "Now, remember, Ty, some days it's gonna rain, and you'll have to take that into account. Sometimes it'll be winter, and there won't be much mowing to do. It's probably better to plan that maybe every other week you're going to be cutting the Flanigans' grass."

Bummer.

"But you know, you can always get more yards."

Aha! I just needed more customers. I started knocking on doors.

Nearly everybody I asked was willing to let me cut their grass. But I knew I had a big problem. I couldn't have my mom come up the street every time I needed to mow a lawn, and I didn't want the fellas to see that I needed my mom to crank the mower.

I called up my cousin Eric, who was a year older, and a lot taller, than me. "Eric, man, I need your help."

"What's that?"

"I've got these customers. I'm getting to cut grass. But I can't … I'm little. I can push the mower, but I can't crank it. But I know you can crank it. So if you come help me, we can just split the money fifty if you're okay with that."

Eric and I started cutting yards together. We ran our little business for about six years before I decided to give it a name: Stop and Stare Lawn Care. The sell was that I would cut your grass so well that people around the community would just stop … and stare. I made up a little flyer and some business cards. I was very artistic as a kid—I drew all the time, did photography, painted. For a while I even thought about being an artist. But when I started making money, mostly what I thought about was continuing to make more money. I had Stop and Stare Lawn Care until I was twenty-one years old, which is to say until I had firmly established myself in the commercial real estate business.

It's not surprising to me now that my mother was the one who planted the seed for me to become an entrepreneur. After all, she was one herself. I didn't pay much attention to it when I was growing up, but at any given time, she was taking care of eight or ten kids at the house. My dad would go to work, my sisters and I would go off to school, and then babies would start coming to the house for day care. My mother got paid by her clients every Friday in cash. She had her own money, and she helped manage the family's money too.

Mom kept kids for over forty years. She was always turning families away—she was that good. She was hardwired to love children with every fiber of her being. Part of the reason I didn't see that activity as part of her entrepreneurial spirit is because she loved it so much. I didn't pick up on the connection that what she loved to do was also how she made money.

Mom was as free as a working person could be; she even took off the entire month of August every year. By comparison with my dad—who clocked in at Lockheed at eight in the morning, clocked out at five, and then drove a taxicab in the evenings—she seemed to have it made.

Both my parents worked extremely hard to take care of us, so much so that I thought we were rich. My mom and dad were working a lot. There was plenty of food always in the refrigerator, and we were able to live in a little brick house just a block from our elementary school. Our family was the first in the neighborhood to get a color television set when they came on the market, and Mom and Dad each had a car.

In the third grade, we started learning about very small and very large amounts—decimal placements on the one hand, lots of commas on the other—and we were taught the concept of a million. I remember the teacher said, "When you're a millionaire, you can do all this wonderful stuff" and then enumerated all the great stuff that millionaires could do.

I came home that day and sat on the front stoop with my dad. "Dad, are we millionaires?" Dad was drinking a little Black Label beer, and he almost spit it out.

"No, no, no, we're not millionaires."

I followed up with "Are we hundred thousandaires?"

"No, no."

"How about thousandaires?"

He paused. "Now, we might be thousandaires."

I'm pretty sure that's the only conversation I ever had with my dad attempting to understand our family's finances. But in my head, I couldn't understand how we were not millionaires in a house so full of everything we needed and so full of love.

I felt that way about our entire Hunter Hills neighborhood too. It seemed like everyone took care of one another, and all the families were friends. My two older sisters were gorgeous girls, so all the big guys in the neighborhood treated me like I was a king. "Hey, Ty! Hey, man! You want some of this?" *This* being candy or assistance with school projects or transportation, or whatever else they had to offer. It wasn't until I was a grown person that I realized they were trying to earn favor with my sisters by offering me treats or help.

My two closest friends were my cousin Eric and my friend Tip, who lived across the street. Besides keeping up with the mowing business, I mostly hung out and played with my friends in the neighborhood. When we came home from school, we'd go over to my house first, and Mom would cook something for us. And then when Tip's mother, Ms. Green, got home from her job as a dental assistant, we'd go over to Tip's and eat again. It was a very close neighborhood—the Greens, the Joneses, the Davises, the Flanigans, and us—and we kids would just be laughing, eating, and doing what happy eight- and nine-year-old little boys do.

One year, my mother presented my dad with the idea of opening a formal day care business—something larger and more professional than her regular operation, maybe even with a few employees. I was in the room when they discussed the possibility, and I remember my dad just shaking his head and saying, "Nah." He had questions about everything—How are we going to do this? How are we gonna do that?—and my mother had an answer for each thing he asked about. But my dad was a pragmatist. He was not going to take risks; that was not in his nature. Working at Lockheed was safe; driving a taxi was safe. My mom keeping kids at home for cash was safe.

That may have been a response my mom could deal with, but later on, when it came time for me to have my first official jobs with W-2s and all, I struggled with Dad's assessment of my prospects.

By the time I started realizing the entrepreneur in me was stronger than my father might have liked, we'd moved from Atlanta to College Park. I was fourteen years old when we left our Atlanta neighborhood, and I understood that it was transforming into an unsafe place. I remember there was a woman from New York—I want to say her name was Sue—who moved into the corner house on our street not long before we left. Tip and I were walking home from school one afternoon, and Sue yelled from her bedroom window, "Call the police! Get the police!" Somebody was in her house at that very moment attempting to rob her. For me, that incident marks the start of things getting bad in the neighborhood I grew up in.

In College Park, I got work at the Steak 'n Shake on Old National, about ten minutes from our new house. Eric and I went up there one day to see if they were hiring, and we got jobs on the spot. Eric got hired to do curb service, taking and delivering customer orders; he was tall, slender, had a big Afro, and was just a good-looking guy. Apparently, I had a face that needed to be kept away from customers, and so I was hired as a dishwasher. There was no training; they just said, "Wash the dishes," and off I went to operate this big industrial-sized machine.

My mom dropped me off for my first shift. I washed dish after dish as if they were each going to be placed in a museum. More and more dishes kept coming through the window, and in a very short while, I could see that I'd gotten in over my head. My shift was supposed to end at eleven o'clock, but I didn't leave until nearly three o'clock in the morning. It got so bad that for a while each of the waitstaff on duty came back to help me.

Of course, my mother was hot when she came to pick me up at eleven o'clock and then had to come back again at three. On the ride home in the middle of the night, she had every word in the world for the management, the lack of employee training, and so on from there. I was just tired and thinking about how I had to be at school at eight in the morning.

During that next week, I learned to wash dishes like nobody's business. I was ready to walk at eleven o'clock sharp, if not much earlier. I even ended up being named employee of the month.

Winners of that award got a certificate and their Polaroid headshot put up on the wall. One of the servers, Cheryl, came up to me a week or so after I'd won that month's award. "Ty, why is your picture not on the wall? Everybody else, when they get employee of the month, their picture is up on the wall the same day." Not until she said it had I thought about it. I had my certificate and my ten-dollar award, and that was okay with me.

I didn't say anything to the manager, but Cheryl did. It meant something to her and to others that I was the first Black employee of the month and the only employee of the month without his photo hanging on the wall. Cheryl called a meeting with the manager and the other Black employees—almost half the staff—and they all gathered around to find out why I hadn't gotten my picture on the wall.

"Well," the manager answered, "we don't know where the camera is."

Cheryl marched over and opened the door to one of the storage rooms. "It's right in here."

They snapped my picture, put it in a little frame, and hung it on the wall for the couple of weeks that remained before another month started and my photo was replaced with another employee's photo—on the very first day. Cheryl walked by my station. "See what I'm saying? You see what I'm saying?" I might still have been naive about race relations at the time, but I was quickly coming to understand the importance of having advocates. Cheryl showed me that people I barely knew would stand up for me and make sure that my dishwasher's face smiled out from its proper place on the wall of honorees.

I had grown up in an all-Black Atlanta neighborhood where everybody knew and looked out for one another, but after we moved to College Park in 1976—from what I could tell, it was an all-white neighborhood until the very day my family moved in—I quickly learned that things had changed dramatically for me, and not for the better. If my life in Atlanta was about being and feeling supported and encouraged everywhere I went and never having to deal with any racially motivated slights, my life in College Park was shaping up to be much the opposite.

I should have known that on the very afternoon we moved into our new house. We were all very excited; the new place had a huge backyard, and I was already planning the games of football and tag that we'd have lots of room to play back there. All five of us stood in the driveway pulling down the doors on the moving truck. When we turned around, we made direct eye contact with the white family across the street—husband, wife, son, daughter, and a golden retriever—looking defiantly at us as the husband pounded a For Sale sign into their front lawn. They had waited for us to turn around and see them, and once the sign was in place, they turned away in unison and marched back into their house.

Up to that point in my life, the only white person I'd known was Ms. Lockwood, the one white teacher at Emma C. Clement Elementary School in Atlanta. She had us reading at an eighth-grade level in our third-grade class. Thanks to her, most of us had also become speed-reading whizzes. To me, Ms. Lockwood was just a regular person like any other, except that she was maybe also an absolute sweetheart. In my mind, if Ms. Lockwood was such a sweet person, surely every other white person would be just the same.

I turned to my dad after the white family across the street retreated into their house. "That's ironic," I offered. "We're moving in, and they're moving out!"

"Boy, get in the house."

My parents and my older sisters recognized what was going on, but not me. I had no clue. As a family, we hadn't talked about race. I hadn't ever seen any hatred directed at people because of their skin color.

About thirty minutes later, I let my parents know that I was headed out to ride my bike around the new neighborhood. Nobody said don't, so I got on my bike and started following the streets that circled the house. I was on Janice Drive and on my way back to the new place when a car pulled up alongside me, driving so slowly it seemed as if we both had stopped.

The windows came down. "Get out of our neighborhood, nigger" came the shouts, and then they started throwing rocks and cans at me. My brain froze for a second, and then I thought, Hey, you got the wrong guy. Whoever did something to you guys, it wasn't me. I literally just moved here.

My heart was beating a hundred miles an hour. I got my focus back and started pedaling as hard as I could. I remember swerving into the driveway of our new house, jumping off, and letting the dropped bike skid on its side toward the carport as I darted inside.

"What's wrong with you, boy?" asked my mom.

"Nothing."

"What's wrong with you, boy?"

"Nothing."

"Boy!"

In the time since, I've described that moment as the first razor blade that I had to swallow. That's the best way I know to say what it felt like. I didn't want to tell my mother. It was dawning on me that I didn't do anything to those boys except be a Black kid riding my bike around the neighborhood.

I was trying to process what was happening, but I was also aware that this was just about the happiest day of my mom's life. I mean, she was so very happy. I had come running into the house seeking safety and stopped short in front of a perfect family tableau—a perfect Norman Rockwell painting. Here was everyone busy at work making the house feel like home—Dad was touching up some paint in the corner, my sisters were putting up the curtains, Mom was unpacking the kitchen—all of them smiling and happy.

I didn't tell my mother what happened. I didn't want to ruin her day. But there would be other razor blades to swallow.

We'd moved mid–school year, so my parents let me finish up the eighth grade back at H. M. Turner High School. Each day after school, I'd go over to a buddy's house and stay there until one of my sisters came to pick me up.

My entire life to that point, I'd walked over the hill and played basketball with the guys on the other side of the street. They were two big families, each with about thirteen kids. Just after we'd moved to College Park, I went over the hill one day to join the other kids on the basketball court. They started throwing the basketball all around me instead of to me. Then one of the guys said, "Get out of the neighborhood, white boy."

I never went back to hang out with them again. By the time I started high school in the fall, I felt pushed out of my old neighborhood and thoroughly unwelcome in my new one. To my Black friends, I was a white boy living in a white neighborhood. To my new schoolmates and neighbors, I was a Black boy undeserving of attention unless it was to be bullied and belittled. I'd transferred from an all-Black high school to a 95 percent white high school. It was very clear and very obvious that they did not want me there.

I remember feeling so angry with my parents. "Why are we here? Why did y'all bring me out here?" It felt unfair that my sisters had gotten to go to high school in the old neighborhood. Why did I have to go to high school with kids who didn't want me around? I wanted to ask those questions but didn't.

For the next few years, I stayed in my room a lot. All I did was go to school, come home, do homework, cut grass. I had no real social life and no new friends. I read a lot, wrote a lot, and worked on my drawing, painting, and photography. Those were my outlets.

As it turned out, College Park was basically a test case for what came to be called "white flight" in America, and I had a front-row seat.

By the time I graduated twelfth grade, the demographics of my high school and our College Park neighborhood had changed dramatically. By then, nearly all the kids in the eighth through the eleventh grades were Black. But that didn't mean that I felt any more welcome than I had when I first arrived.

One thing I didn't do was extrapolate from those early experiences of racism to any set of assumptions about white people in general. That nasty family across the street didn't know us, didn't understand the first thing about us. Those boys throwing cans and rocks from their car were just three assholes.

Earlier, I pointed out that I'm hardwired to see for myself—especially when it comes to other people. Even to this day, and with far greater awareness of how systemic racism structures our human interactions, I still want to get to know people, really know them, even if they seem to others, as Schwartz did to many, to be either a racist or an asshole.

I may have turned inward during those rough years in high school, but I did not end up shutting down.

In fact, by the time I graduated high school, my entrepreneurial spirit was budding again, this time coming up against my father's far more pragmatic preferences and advice. My dad was what people used to refer to as a man's man. He was in the army, an Eighty-Second Airborne paratrooper who'd joined the military when he was just fourteen. When, at nineteen, I finally figured out what I wanted to be when I grew up and came home to tell my parents, let's just say that my dad was not enthusiastic.

"Dad, I figured out what I'm going to do the rest of my life. I'm going to be a commercial real estate broker."

"Okaaay."

"A man by the name of Mr. Thomas W. Tift with Atlanta Air Center Realty offered me a job to come work with him."

"How much is he gonna pay you?"

"Well, it's straight commission. So, you know, it's unlimited. But I got to do the work."

Dad gave me an "oh my God" headshake. "What kind of benefits is he offering?"

"Well, Dad, I have to buy my own benefits."

Then my father said something completely out of character. "Well, I want to meet this guy before you go to work for him."

I obeyed and arranged the meeting. My dad and Mr. Tift greeted one another with a warm handshake, then took seats on opposite sides of the conference table. My dad launched into his questions: How much would my son be paid? What kind of benefits would he receive? Apparently, my earlier answers had been insufficient. My father needed to go to the source for his information.

Mr. Tift explained, "This is traditionally a straight commission business, but there are no limits. If Dallas does well, the company does well, and that means we all do well. He's going to have to buy his own benefits, because that's how the commission business is set up …"

My dad stood up, then Mr. Tift stood up as my dad reached over to shake his hand. "I'm going to trust you with my son," he said, looking Mr. Tift straight on. I felt like a bride being given away at the altar.

"He's in good hands." Tift smiled.

After that, I didn't look back. I started making money hand over fist. I ended up buying a second car. I was living in my parents' house, so of course my father wanted to know "What the hell are you doing with two cars?"

I moved into an apartment with a friend and joined the Atlanta Metropolitan Cathedral. Not long after that, I got married. Soon after, we had a child. And soon after that, we got divorced. I wanted to have a steady enough income to pay $750 a month in child support, so I went looking for a second job. I got three offers on the same day: one was working at the post office, the next working at the airport keying in car tags, and the third one I don't even remember. In Dad's opinion, it was clear that I should take the job at the Hapeville post office, the main post office in Atlanta—it was a steady job with great benefits. That wasn't the job I wanted, but, feeling the pull of my dad's pragmatism, I showed up for orientation anyway.

Picture two hundred thousand square feet of people sorting mail with the help of giant machines. Everyone was seated and quiet, sorting at warp speed, hands shuffling left to right, left to right, the machines humming. Everyone looked a bit, if not a lot, out of shape, and all of them were smoking. I started imagining myself getting comfortable sitting there with them, aging a good twenty years in my first couple of months on the job. Just watching them, I felt trapped. No way in hell could I do this! I imagined a slow death by paper cuts and inactivity.

I understood the importance of having benefits and of receiving a paycheck twice a month. But the airport job seemed so much better; if I could finish the work in an hour, they'd still pay me for the full eight-hour shift. I could work outside and on my own, still having to clock in and out, but it felt freer to me.

No question, I was choosing the airport job.

The entrepreneur in me already knew well that I always had a better way of doing something. At the very least, the airport job would allow me to be the one who determined how best and how quickly I could work. In earlier jobs, I'd already proven myself to be a nuisance, always seeing alternatives and always asking, "Why don't we do it like this?" I was very much the same as my mother in that way, always strategizing about improvements. Far into her life, she was asking those sorts of questions, and today, far into my own life, I see that I'm still asking those questions too. I'm constantly

I know that if I ever utter the words "This is just how we do it here," I'm finished.

trying to learn more, to figure out how someone went about making something new and interesting happen. I've been in the commercial real estate field for over forty years now, and I'm still committed to being better tomorrow than I am today. I know that if I ever utter the words "This is just how we do it here," I'm finished.

Just as much as I like to figure out why things are as they are, I despise being the only one willing to do the hard work.

At the Steak 'n Shake job, typically there would be at least two people working the grill, one person taking orders, a dishwasher, four or five indoor servers, another three working curbside, and a manager all present during the same shift—at least a dozen people at any given time. One afternoon, I clocked in at four o'clock just as the other shift left, and there was no one else there with me for a full ninety minutes. Customers hadn't suddenly stopped appearing, so what did I do? I got on the grill and the fryer. I made milkshakes and manned both the drive-through window and the inside counter. I took customer payments. I'd seen everyone else do their jobs a million times over. So I just ran the entire restaurant by myself.

Our manager at the time, Linda, should have been there an hour before the four o'clock shift. When she finally arrived, she apologized for being late. In that moment, I had no words for her. By the time she arrived, other employees had also started coming in for their shifts. I went back to washing dishes. When I left that night, Linda stopped me on my way out the door. "Ty, I just want to say thank you."

My middle sister is five years older than me, and when I wasn't getting ready for work at the usual time the next day, she noticed. "Ty, you going to work today?"

She wasn't expecting my answer. "No. I'm going to quit."

"What are you going to tell Daddy?"

"I ain't telling Daddy!"

"Oh. Well, how are you going to do it?"

"Watch me." I picked up the phone.

"Hey, Ty" came Linda's voice on the line.

"Linda, I will not be in today."

"Oh, you're not feeling well?"

"I'm feeling fine."

"What do you mean?"

"Linda, last night I had to run that place by myself, doing thirteen different jobs. Nobody said anything to me except 'thank you.'" I went on: "I can't work at a place that doesn't run properly. I did every job because I've watched everybody do their jobs. I know how to do this so well that I could run the place. I literally ran the place for an hour and a half by myself."

I wasn't finished. "Let me tell you this: I'm tired of coming home smelling like onions and a milkshake. I'm just tired of it. There's something better for me than this hamburger bullshit."

I hung up the phone, and in that moment, my sister's expression matched her words perfectly. "Ooohhhh. You're going to be in trouble!"

I waited a couple of days before telling my father.

"You quit the job? Don't nobody quit! You don't quit a job! You don't ever burn any bridges!"

"Dad, I'm going to have another job. I've got an interview at Richway tomorrow."

"You don't ever quit a job till you have another job to go to!"

He was hot. But I knew my mother would have done the same thing as me.

I ended up getting the job at Richway the next day. It didn't matter to my father, though. I had to hear over and over again for several months about how I should never quit a job without having another, better job firmly in place.

After Richway, I worked for a time at J. Riggins clothing store. I figured that if I had enough money to be able to buy clothes I liked, I should work someplace that sold clothes I liked and offered an employee discount.

It was at J. Riggins that I came to understand that I was a great salesman.

Riggins wasn't a super expensive place, but it was a busy place where people came for suits at a $120 price point. One day, a couple came in who reminded me of how much my mother's influence had made me the young man I'd become. In comes a very prim and proper white woman with a husband who looked to me like a dog on a leash. She wanted him to have some nicer suits. I brought out all the basics, explaining, "You'll want to have a navy suit; you'll want to have a black suit …" and on I went, presenting a host of options for improving the fellow's appearance.

In the end, he tried on a dozen different suits, and I made the biggest sale I'd ever made at J. Riggins. As the couple was checking out, I asked the wife, because she was the one paying for everything, "If you don't mind, may I ask what you do for a living?"

"I am in real estate," she answered.

"Oh, you know, I'm thinking of getting into real estate—commercial real estate."

"Oh. You'll never make it. You'll never make it." She didn't stop there. "You're Black, and you're young. You may make it in residential, but you'll never make it in commercial."

Mind you, I'm checking out the biggest J. Riggins tab I've ever seen and feeling pretty damned good about it. As I focused on getting all the codes entered correctly into the register, I thought, Have you met me? I don't think you know me.

Looking back on moments like that, I thank God for my mother, who was constantly lifting me up and telling me that I could do whatever I wanted.

I remember coming home from elementary school, running into the kitchen, and crying to my mother, "Mom! The kids at school called me Pinocchio! They said I have a skinny body and a big nose!"

She stopped washing dishes and turned to look over at me. "Son, you have the nose of a king." Then she turned her attention right back to washing the plate in her hand.

I ran to the bathroom to have a look in the mirror. She was right! I'd never noticed it before, but I did have the nose of a king!

Mom's words always stuck with me just like that, through the entirety of my youth. And she offered those encouraging words on the regular. I might've been fourteen when we took a trip to New York City to visit my aunt—my very first trip to the city—and I had a helluva lot of questions about everything we were seeing. At one point, my aunt turned to me, exasperated. "You're asking too many questions, Ty!"

My mother let her get ahead of us. "You ask as many questions as you like. That's the only way you're going to learn. You continue to ask questions, Ty."

Well before I understood the extent and value of what she'd done, my mother had wrapped a layer of Teflon all around me. Words that might have been intended to hurt me never really stuck because my mother made sure that I knew well the narrative in which I was royalty, was authorized to ask whatever I wanted, and could choose my path from a whole world of opportunities.

My heart goes out to the kids whose parents told them the opposite, that they weren't nothin' or that they weren't ever going to be enough. I didn't know about all the ways in which I was an underdog because I had parents who didn't allow me to know it. My mother told me that I could do anything that I wanted to do, and I thoroughly believed her. She'd been raised by her grandmother, who was born a slave and who learned to read and helped grow a big church community. My great-grandmother always told my mother, "There's a big, beautiful world out there, and you can do in it whatever it is you want to do."

I believed my mother's pronouncements so much that I confidently entered an industry with fewer than 1 percent in 1982 of people who looked like me. Now, staying in that industry wasn't just my mother's doing. I was also the product of Schwartz's endless encouragement. They both saw the same thing in me, and I'm forever grateful to them for lifting me up, each getting me to a different place in my life.

If my mother was the source of the entrepreneur in me, my father was the source of my commitment to hard work, to taking advantage of opportunities offered, and to making sacrifices that are necessary for success and longevity in a career. Just as I'd mimicked and learned

> **You've got to figure out how to get over or around or through whatever mountains are in your path.**

from both Schwartz and Stanley, I'd also picked up qualities from both my mother and father—each one balancing out the other. As with Stanley, so too with my dad: both understood that you've got to figure out how to get over or around or through whatever mountains are in your path. The worst thing you can do is decide to sit down in front of that mountain and wait for something to happen or someone to come rescue you.

CHAPTER 2

Klan Killer

I didn't always know what I wanted to be when I grew up. But I knew two things for certain: I wanted to make some money, and I didn't want to leave Atlanta. I am an Atlanta boy, and as *Ralph from Ben Hill* would say: I'm Atlanta born, Atlanta bred, and when I die, I'll be Atlanta dead.

What I knew at age nineteen was that I was already five years behind where I needed to be when it came to thinking about my career. I knew that for a fact because back when I was fourteen, I'd witnessed two siblings from my high school—Troy and Stacy—map out and debate the details of their entire lives. I'd just met them at my new high school, Lakeshore, after we moved to College Park. I had gone over to their house one afternoon thinking we might all go out in the yard to play ball, but what I witnessed instead was the two of them engaged in intense back-and-forth banter about their plans. One was going to become an anesthesiologist and an air force pilot, and the other intended to become a dentist. They had made vision boards on the walls above their beds with Morehouse College pennants, photos of the cars they planned to buy, and timelines for when they would reach goal markers on the path to achieving their dreams. One was debating the other about the timeline of being able to afford a black Porsche 911: "You won't be able to afford that car! You'll just be in your residency!"

At the time, Troy and Stacy didn't know how pivotal that afternoon had been for me. I left their house thinking, Ty, you are woefully unprepared. You're a loser. You don't have a plan. What are you doing? You've been here fourteen whole years, and you have nothing to show for it. Walking home, I thought over my whole life. Their dad had pushed them to dream big and make solid plans. Nobody in my family had pushed me like that. If I graduated high school and got a good job at the post office, my family would be perfectly happy.

That same year, Malcolm Forbes started publishing what would become an annual list of the four hundred wealthiest people in the United States. So to help move myself along, I picked up a copy of *Forbes* magazine and looked at each person on the list to see how they had become so wealthy. At that time, nearly all four hundred of those people did at least one of four things: they were in real estate, the oil industry, or the burgeoning technology industry, or they'd been successful working on the stock exchange.

Looking over these four categories, I reasoned that I'd likely need to be in Houston, Texas, if I wanted to make money in oil. Stocks meant moving to Chicago or New York. Technology could have worked but seemed antithetical to my personality—"too geeky" was my thought at the time. That left real estate, and my very first thought about that was "No way am I gonna drive people around in my car and work on weekends," so that knocked out residential. That meant I'd have to choose commercial real estate. From what I could tell, that would be far more of a nine-to-five gig, and with a more corporate feel.

Next, I did some additional research. Was there anyone who looked like me in the commercial real estate business in Atlanta? I'd heard of a guy over at Coldwell Banker, so I reached out to him several times but never heard back. Luckily for me, my sister Gigi was dating Michael Hightower, a College Park City Council member and the most influential person I knew. When I asked Michael if he knew of anyone in commercial real estate, he put me in touch with Bill Culmer, who ran his own company and who gave me permission to shadow one of his retail brokers, Steve Gaultney. On the day I shadowed Steve, he took me to a meeting where he was representing a big-name eyeglasses company preparing to enter the Atlanta market.

I sat quietly for some minutes, watching Steve negotiate with his client. They shook hands over the deal, and just as quickly, we left.

"Do you have any questions about that meeting, Dallas?"

I thought, I don't really know what just happened, but what I said out loud was, "It looked like you started off at a tough spot, but you shook hands at the end, and it seemed to go better, so I assume you agreed on something and wrapped up the deal."

"Yeah, yeah, we did."

"So I only have one question. How much money are you gonna make on this deal?"

Steve laughed. "Thirty thousand."

This was 1982. The median household annual income for a family of four at that time was $28,000. I'd just watched this dude make that on one transaction. Yeah, commercial real estate was the business for me. But Steve could not help me any further.

"Dallas, we're a really small firm. We don't have any room to hire new brokers."

"I understand. I am very appreciative, you know, for you taking me with you today."

Steve took me to lunch, where he introduced me to a young white guy, Tom Thompson, who was training at Culmer. Tom was also a student at Georgia State, so we chatted about our courses and exchanged numbers. Not more than a couple of days later, Tom called me with a tip that Tommy Tift Jr. at Atlanta Air Center Realty was looking to hire and train someone in the business.

I said, "Tommy Tift as in Tift County, city of Tifton, Tift College?"

And Tom replied, "One and the same."

I'd later learn that Mr. Tift had said to Tom, "I'm looking for someone just like you." Tom Thompson told Mr. Tift that he would have his friend give Mr. Tift a call. I assumed that my given name—Tonialo—was likely to keep me from getting hired by someone from south Georgia with roots that deep. I imagined Tonialo Smith's résumé ending up in file thirteen, headed straight to the trash can.

Back in high school, I'd worked on the yearbook staff as head of photography. I was responsible for things like ordering film and selecting images. At that time, Kodak was a major carrier of camera film, but there was a new company, Fujifilm, that was trying to get business from our high school. As one of the big football games approached, I'd scheduled eight photographers to work the game, but we hadn't yet gotten the film we needed from Kodak. I called up the Kodak rep and read him the riot act. I even threatened that if he didn't have the film to us by two thirty that afternoon, he could forget our contract, and we would sign with Fujifilm instead.

Now, one of the young ladies on the staff, Sharnette Mitchell, happened to hear my sixteen-year-old self on the phone with the Kodak rep.

"Wow! You sound just like J. R.!" J. R. Ewing was the name of a scheming oil tycoon on the hit show *Dallas*.

I smiled and joked, "J. R. ain't got shit on me. You call me Dallas, 'cause I'm badder than the whole show!"

After graduating high school in 1980, my friend Chuck Moss and I went together to Tennessee State. We'd spent the first part of that year listening to everyone around us talk about the schools they'd gotten accepted to, the ones they'd chosen, but neither of us had applied anywhere. One afternoon when we were sitting around together, I asked, "Chuck, man, are you going to college?"

"I don't know. You going to college?"

I didn't know, but then I said, "Man, let's do this."

We walked over to the library to consult the college directory—a big book listing every college and important features of each.

"This is what we're going to do," I said. "We're going to open this book to a random page, point a finger at the page, and whatever school it is we're pointing at, we're just going to send off our applications and see if we get in. If we get in, then God meant for us to go to college. If we don't get in, then it's just not meant to be."

"Okay!" Chuck agreed.

We landed on Tennessee State University in Nashville. Chuck got accepted first, and I got accepted a week later—which was about two weeks out from when freshmen were expected to arrive on campus. I needed to inform the family.

"Dad, I got accepted, and I want to go to Tennessee State!"

"Huh?"

I told him what it would cost and which grants I was eligible for. My dad said that if I did well, he'd buy me a car.

On move-in day, Chuck and I each got dropped off by our parents at about the same time, and Chuck was already hungry. "Ty, let's go over to the cafeteria."

"Hey, man, don't call me Ty," I answered. "Call me Dallas."

Chuck didn't miss a beat. "All right, Dallas. Let's go to the cafeteria."

Dallas got straight As freshman year and got a brand new car the following summer—a Fiat X1/9, a little two-seater with a targa top. That car was a chick magnet. Through the summer and during fall semester sophomore year, I thoroughly made up for being a nerd the year prior. That first quarter with my new wheels, my GPA dropped from a 4.0 to a 2.8.

My sister Gigi was working at Georgia State at the time, so I called her up. "Gigi, what average do you have to have to transfer to Georgia State?"

"A two point five."

"Okay, help me transfer now while I've got a two point eight, because next quarter I'll probably be below that."

We never told my dad what happened. The only thing he said was "You come back home, you're going to be paying for your own tuition." Thankfully, Georgia State was only $333 a quarter. I graduated in 1986, and for my education there, all in, I think I paid $5,600. Today GSU is one of the top business schools in the country, so that was one of the best investments I ever made.

> Today GSU is one of the top business schools in the country, so that was one of the best investments I ever made.

It was after I'd returned to Georgia that I had the opportunity to call on Mr. Tift to ask for work. I'd already decided not to use my given first name, so I played around with several versions until I settled on T. Dallas Smith, which came from thinking about business magnate T. Boone Pickens—one of the names on the Forbes 400 list. Next, I edited my résumé, leaving off my basketball and track experience and keeping all the white-looking activities like tennis and chess. On paper, I looked like a six-foot-two, blond, blue-eyed white boy from Texas.

Mr. Tift told Tom Thompson that he was impressed with my résumé. On the telephone call to set up an in-person meeting, I was careful to use my whitest white-man-in-America voice, which for me was the voice of original *The Tonight Show* host Johnny Carson. When I showed up for the interview, the young woman sitting at the front desk, Susan Christy, politely asked if she could help me.

"Yes, I'm here to see Mr. Tift."

"Do you have an appointment?"

"Yes, I do. I'm his two o'clock appointment, Dallas Smith."

Susan's entire body shifted away from me as she looked up at my face. If there hadn't been a wall immediately behind her, she might have flipped over in her chair.

"Hold on one minute, please." She stood and walked backward, facing me, her index finger pointing straight in the air, into Mr. Tift's office, eventually closing the door between us.

Later, I would learn exactly what she said when the door was closed. "Mr. Tift. Dallas is here, and he's Black."

Tift's reply: "Well, since he's here, let him come on in. This will be the shortest interview in the history of mankind."

Susan emerged. "He'll see you now."

In his office, Mr. Tift and I shook hands, exchanged some pleas-antries. Before taking my seat, I noticed a picture of Ronald Reagan on his desk. "Oh, you're a Reagan fan?"

"Yes."

"So am I!"

His eyes grew round with surprise.

"He was the first president I voted for."

Let me say this right here: I became a Republican in the early 1980s because I'd come to admire Schwartz, and Schwartz was a Republican. When I came of voting age, Jimmy Carter was running against Ronald Reagan. Jimmy Carter is from Georgia and a very nice man, but the one thing I knew about him was that during his administration interest rates were 18 to 19 percent. So I went for the other guy. It wasn't a blue or red thing, like it is now. For me, at the time, it was just a vote for the guy with lower rates.

Tift and I talked Reagan and economic policy for an hour.

"You play tennis?" I inquired, noticing that he and I had the same black graphite racket—a fairly new item on the market.

We talked tennis for another hour. We had more things in common than things that separated us.

"What do you want to get paid?" Tift asked.

"Mr. Tift. I am not worried about money right now. I want to learn this business and get to the point where I can take care of myself. I'll work straight commission."

He smiled. "Okay."

We shook hands, and I left.

I'd later learn that Tift came out of his office and said to Susan, "I'm gonna do something I thought I'd never do. I'm going to hire that young man."

And he did. That same day, he called me to say as much.

"Mr. Tift, I'd like to start next week, because I want to go to Mardi Gras."

He laughed out loud and told me that his daughter would be going to Mardi Gras too.

The next week, my training with Mr. Tift went like this: His family owned over four hundred thousand square feet of industrial space, thirty thousand square feet of office space, and another three thousand square feet of retail space—all on property adjacent to the Atlanta airport. I came into the business as Tift's exclusive leasing guy. He drove me around, showed me the buildings, then handed me a folder with a list of the people he wanted to attract as tenants in his building.

That was it. I got a desk to sit at and a phone for making calls. I didn't know shit, but I picked up that phone and assumed that I'd figure it out as I went along.

I was young and hungry, so I figured it out pretty quickly. I got my first deal in under three months—a taxicab company leasing one of the buildings across a railway track that ran through the property. My commission on that deal was $300, but you'd have thought I made $3 million. What mattered most was having proved to myself that I could do the work. I could earn money just talking. I had shown the property and met with the prospect. I didn't have to own anything. I could just make calls and close on deals.

My first year, I made $6,000; my second, $12,000; and I doubled my salary almost every year from that point forward. And all the while, I was a college student living at home with my mom and dad.

When I started working for him, Mr. Tift didn't have a Black person filling any role in his business. Nobody Black worked for him, not even the cleaning staff. From what I could tell, that was a long-standing generational habit. But when Mr. Tift met me, we became friends. More than that—to this day, we treat one another like family.

It wasn't until the latter years I spent working for Mr. Tift that I got introduced to his father, "Big Tift," as I called him. Big Tift had clearly been a tough dude in the past but was now in his nineties, nearly doubled over, powered by an external oxygen tank, and receiving twenty-four-hour nurse assistance. When he came to the office one day, he pulled up in the biggest Cadillac I'd ever seen with a personalized "TIFT" license plate registered in Tift County, Georgia. His driver and nurse helped him out of the car and into the building. Everyone scrambled. "Tift is here! Tift is here!"

With his nurse just a few steps behind him guiding the oxygen tank, Big Tift entered the office. Mr. Tift bent down so he could speak right into his father's ear, and in a very loud voice announced, "Daddy, I want you to meet our new marketing director, Dallas Smith." Mind you, Big Tift was severely bent over, so all he could see were my shoes and pants. He reached his hand out in front of him toward me. I took his hand in mine, and that was when he gasped aloud—his oxygen machine beeping rapidly—and stood straight as if his back had snapped into position like a newly sprung hinge.

"All right, then, Daddy. I know you've got to go." Mr. Tift turned his attention to the nurse. She was already working the machine to ensure that Big Tift was getting enough air. Mr. Tift, Susan, and I were standing at the door waving to the little group as they loaded Big Tift back into the car and drove off. "I haven't seen him stand up straight in ten years," Mr. Tift marveled.

Two weeks later, we got word that Big Tift had died.

"You know, you killed him," Susan teased. "You didn't just kill any man, Dallas. You killed the Grand Dragon of the Tift County Ku Klux Klan."

Working for Mr. Tift and discovering what we did and didn't have in common wasn't without its difficulties. His appreciation of me eventually became a problem insofar as it affected his relationship with one of his sons. I won't get into the details of that conflict—his son and I have since mended our relationship—but suffice it to say that I ended up quitting my job and not speaking with Mr. Tift for several years.

Thankfully, I had a mentor, Roy Ludwig, who'd sold his firm Barton and Ludwig to CBRE—that sale was how CBRE had made its way into the Atlanta market. Roy had let me interview him during a "fireside chat" series with the Metropolitan Business Association—MBA for short—a gathering I'd started at Atlanta Metropolitan Cathedral. MBA was a Christian businessmen's group that focused on informing aspiring entrepreneurs; our tagline was "Come get your MBA." After that event, Roy became a great advisor and behind-the-scenes helper to me. When I consulted him about the problems that had arisen with Mr. Tift, Roy said plainly, "You know, Dallas, once trust is lost, it's hard to get back."

I was probably thirty by the time I got back in touch with the man who had welcomed me into his business and given me a solid start to my career. The reason I got back in touch? Whenever people would ask me the story of how I got into the business, I would tell them about how Mr. Tift had hired me and given me the opportunity of a lifetime.

Telling that story without being in contact with Mr. Tift felt like lying.

So I picked up the phone. "Mr. Tift, I know we haven't been talking. But I want you to know how much I value you bringing me into the real estate business. None of the work I've had since would have come to me if it hadn't been for you."

He apologized. We made up. That was half my life ago, and we've met up for lunch or dinner nearly once every quarter since.

I truly believe that my relationship with Mr. Tift helped him realize that Big Tift had told him lies about Black people. I take as evidence the fact that Mr. Tift hired a Black accountant and other Black employees in his company and welcomed Black tenants into his buildings. It's also something that he and I have addressed in conversation. I remember he once said to me, "You're just different than most Black people."

I thanked God for common sense and patience as I replied, "Mr. Tift, how many Black people do you know?"

"You and Mammy." Mammy was the woman who'd raised him.

"Mr. Tift, I imagine you loved Mammy?"

"Yeah. I loved Mammy."

"And you love me."

"Yeah. I love you."

"Now imagine if you met five more Black people, and you ended up liking them, too, even loving them. Just imagine that."

I could see from the expression on his face that the thought had never crossed his mind. To him, I was a special creature, an exception to a rule.

"Mr. Tift, I'm a human being like everybody else. I've got my flaws; you've got yours. But you like me, and I like you. It's really that simple. We each meet other people—some of them we like, some of them we don't, right?"

"Dallas, you're right."

When people ask me what I'm proudest of in my career, often they'll make the assumption that it's my latest, biggest, or most attention-getting deal. But they're not even close. The thing I'm consistently most proud of is the fact that I've witnessed people change right before my eyes. The son of a KKK Grand Dragon met a guy like me, and that changed both his heart and his actions.

I've said that my mother was an independent thinker; she raised me to go find out for myself about situations and about people. I saw her do it, and I'm happy to have inherited that same habit from her. Continuing that practice means that I can say from my own personal experience, I know love does conquer all. With Mr. Tift and with others, I've gotten to be the person who helps change someone else's opinions. I've gotten to be the one who helps to break a chain of dangerous thoughts and behaviors. The same

I know love does conquer all.

way I came to adore Schwartz was how I came to adore Mr. Tift—I got to know them. If I'd let someone else tell me about them and never seen for myself, I'd never have learned that we had lots in common, lots of good reasons to connect.

I'm not trying to say that this has always been my experience with the people I've met. Far from it, especially when it comes to people who don't look like me. But I'll keep putting myself out there, looking for connections, with the idea that if someone else doesn't receive me, that's on them. It won't be because I didn't offer them all of me or didn't let them really meet me and learn who I am.

Over and over, I see how other people are surprised by my interest in finding out about them or hearing their story. And people are always a bit surprised when our stories end up having many points of similarity. Those might seem, at first, like superficial connections—we like a particular kind of music; we each have three daughters; we've traveled to the same places—but I'm always looking for what we have in common. That's something we can build on. And the next time I see that person, we have a closer relationship than we did before.

CHAPTER 3

Black Asset

During the recession of 1987, real estate shifted from a landlords' market to a tenants' market. One of the opportunities that Mr. Tift had provided for me was that we started a tenant representation firm—First Brokerage. Tift had a management company called First Management at the time, so I thought the new firm's name made sense, and he liked it. When it was time for me to leave Tift, I knew that tenant representation was where I needed to be.

Thanks to Michael Lomax, another Atlanta politician, I was able to get an interview at Carter & Associates, which was the number one brokerage firm in Atlanta in 1989. Cushman & Wakefield, which was owned by the Rockefellers, was number two, and in my mind, I needed to be at the number one or the number two firm. There were, of course, no brothers at either organization. When I met with Ben Carter, he was forthright. Thirty minutes into the

> I knew how to overcome objections. But overcoming the objection to me being Black? I had no way to overcome that.

interview he said, "We're not ready for a Black broker." Having worked in sales for quite some time, I knew how to overcome objections. But overcoming the objection to me being Black? I had no way to overcome that. So I stood up, shook his hand, thanked him for his time, and left.

That meant setting my sights on Cushman & Wakefield.

Michael Elting was running their Atlanta office at the time. By this time, too, my résumé was killing it. I'd done multimillion-dollar deals; I'd done incredible volume by myself at a small firm; I'd done everything from industrial to office to retail to land. But when Mike interviewed me, I could tell that he was going through the motions without real interest.

The interview process was set up so that I had to meet with lots of people who worked in the office—brokers, secretaries, nearly everyone. Four months went by, and I was still interviewing for that job.

One morning, while on my knees saying my prayers, I felt that God was telling me, "Get up and go to work." So I got dressed in a crisp white shirt, power tie, and blue suit and went down to the Cushman & Wakefield office. I'd been there so many times that the receptionist, Myra, greeted me like an old friend. "Hey, Dallas. How are you doing?"

"I am good, Myra. How are you?"

"I'm good, Dallas. Who you here to see today?"

"Well, I want to see if Mike Elting is around."

"Oh, you have an appointment?"

"No, Myra. I don't have an appointment."

"Okay, let me just see. Let me put a call back ... Dallas, he's in a meeting right now. Give him some minutes. You have time?"

"Yeah, I have time."

I sat down, and we chatted a bit. Then the regional president, Bill Bugg, came down the hallway toward us. Before he got near, Myra whispered, "Dallas, do you know Bill Bugg?"

"I know who he is, but I haven't met him yet." It was amazing that I hadn't met Bill, considering that I'd gotten to know just about everyone else in the entire place.

He approached. Myra offered, "Mr. Bugg? I have somebody here who has a mutual friend of yours, and I am not sure if you two have met."

"And who is that, Myra?"

"Dallas Smith. You two have a mutual friend."

Bill looked down at me. "Who's your friend?"

"Roy Ludwig."

Roy was serious about his Christianity and had pointed out to me that he understood it as a white man's duty to help Blacks, since their current condition was the product of white men's efforts. Roy had shared with me that God had told him he needed to mentor ten Black men and get ten of his white friends to do the same.

"Dallas," he asked, "how many of my friends do you think I've been able to convince to do that?"

He touched the tips of his fingers and thumbs together in the shape of a big goose egg.

But that hadn't stopped him. Roy Ludwig was that dude, out there mentoring and quietly helping Black men move up in the world.

Bill recognized Roy's name. "Oh yes, of course. What's going on with you, Dallas?"

"Well, I'm not sure. That's what I'm here to find out."

"You got a minute? Why don't you come on back to my office?"

Bill and I talked for a good hour.

"Dallas, let me tell you. People ask me why we don't have any Black brokers at Cushman & Wakefield. There are two schools of thought: one is that we can't find any qualified Black brokers, and the other is that we don't want them."

I nodded.

"The reality is that we don't want them."

He leaned in, put his hand on my shoulder, and said, "But there is no reason why you shouldn't be the first."

I was twenty-six years old. I had a wife and a baby on the way. I wasn't trying to be the Dr. King or Malcolm X of commercial real estate. I was just eager to take care of my own. Honestly, looking back on that time, I think that if I had been working on making my way in the business and thinking about how to take care of other people like me, I would not have made it. There was so much that I was learning and so much that I still didn't understand.

After that conversation with Bill Bugg, I started working for Cushman & Wakefield as their first Black broker. Unlike when anyone else joined the firm, there was no press release with a corresponding headshot announcing my hire. There were about forty other brokers, and I mostly looked after myself. I made friends with Steve Parrot in the research department. He wasn't a broker, but he was a genuinely nice guy, just good people. And I made friends with James Arnold, the shoeshine man in the building.

James was really the only Black person in the building I could go and talk to. Cushman's offices were in the old IBM tower, and IBM was a really stodgy computer company. On their casual Fridays, they were given permission to wear blue shirts with their suits instead of white ones. The whole building had essentially followed suit—there was a silk-stocking law firm, our firm, and a handful of other stuffy companies. There were not a lot of Black people in the building; some of the security guards were Black, but even they were extremely buttoned up.

James could see that I didn't much like that buttoned-up culture, and he helped me through a lot of days during the six years I spent working there. No matter what I was going through, he listened and then passed on some words of encouragement. "Go on up there and whup their ass," he'd say, giving me that little bit of energy I needed to get back to the job. To this day I tell people, "Even professional teams need cheerleaders. Those guys might be making millions, but their bank accounts alone aren't enough. People need cheerleaders, no matter what." James was that guy for me, hands down, and we're still really good friends now. In fact, his brother works at my firm. I tease his brother all the time that the only reason he got a job working for me was because his brother James is so amazing.

As I got the lay of the land at Cushman, I could more clearly see the typical dynamic: all these white boys hanging out, going around giving deals to one another. Being social with one another was also how they learned about each other's projects and got invited in on them. And working on deals together was what solidified their friendships, making them better and better friends who would then bring each other in on more and more deals.

I was heavily into the church at that time, and more than a couple of the guys I worked with at Cushman were Christians. In my head, they were my brothers, precisely because we were all Christians. I was so disappointed with my brothers, and I found myself thinking about how these guys called themselves Christians, but their attitudes toward me were much the same as American white men's attitudes toward Black men had been for a very long time. These were not guys who would come to my aid or stand with me if I needed them.

I had managed to become the first Black broker at a very white firm, but that had only made it clearer to me how white men treat a Black man when he makes his way into their territory. That was a very low point for me, and I remember seriously questioning whether commercial real estate was really the career I wanted. Would I always have to put up with this behavior if I chose to stay? I even wrote a poem, trying to make sense of my conflicted feelings and my colleagues' behaviors.

TEARS OF BLACK FOLK

May 1996

The tears of Black Folk could equal
every pond, lake, river, stream,
creek, ocean; every wet spot there is
on this planet, and there would still be
tears remaining. Why? For being
forsaken by each other, our brother,
our other brother that is. Tears! For
every injustice, and Lord knows there
have been many. Tears! For not
getting the benefit of the doubt.
Tears! For doing better than most
and still not being good enough.
Tears! For being. Tears! For
dreaming. Tears! For surviving.
Tears! For being judged collectively
and not individually.

> Sometimes, I understand why the
> sweet by and by is so sweet.
> Sometimes I want to give up, but I
> know that will only prove their case.
> So, I persist, and believe that just
> around the corner there will be no
> more tears.

I've never shared that poem with anyone until deciding to include it here. And that's because I want to be clear about my experience, about the opposition that I faced in those early years and would continue to face—the opposition that I expect other people like me to still face in this industry and many others. If you're a Black person with dreams, your life is not likely to be easy. There will be tears.

But looking back on those words from my younger days, I see that I didn't give up the faith that just around the corner, those tears might be no more. Down as I was at that point, I was still hopeful. And today, I'm still hopeful. It's been that thread of hopefulness—thinner at some moments, thicker at others—that has motivated me to encourage other Black people to find their way in this industry.

It's been that thread of hopefulness—thinner at some moments, thicker at others—that has motivated me to encourage other Black people to find their way in this industry.

There were times when the only person who was going to determine whether or not I stuck with my dreams was me. And I thank God I didn't quit.

One of those white guys I mentioned—named Mark Christopher—was a tall, blond, blue-eyed broker, a good Christian, and a very smart, very nice guy. When I decided to try to bridge the barrier between me and the other brokers by bringing people in on my deals, Mark was the man I approached. I had made a deal for a small space, maybe two hundred square feet, with a young lady who owned an education company. About four months after we made that arrangement, her little company got purchased by Jostens, and she called to ask for more space and for me to be her broker on the deal. I figured she might need a couple more offices, but instead, she asked for forty thousand square feet. When she called, she made sure to tell me that I had been the only broker at a large and well-known company who'd been willing to take care of her original small-space deal.

When she gave me my first significant deal at Cushman, I invited Mark to help me with it, and we split the six-figure commission fifty-fifty. I can't remember the second deal I brought him in on, but what I do remember is that after that second deal, it was time to make my case.

"Mark, I see you doing deals with some of the other brokers. I've brought you in on two deals now, but, dude, you haven't brought me in on anything."

"Yeah."

"What have I got to do to get brought in? You're a Christian, right? I'm a Christian, too, and we are supposed to be brothers. I see you helping everybody else. Now I am bringing you deals. You and I are more like brothers than you and anybody else who might look like you in this place. You should bring your brother in on something."

"You're right, Dallas."

He turned to his desk and brought out two deals for us to work on together. Mark and I ended up having a great relationship, one that ended too soon. Eighteen months later, he was dead from a fast-growing lung cancer. Since 1998, the year he died, the annual real estate brokers' Atlanta prayer breakfast has been conducted in his honor.

In the late eighties and early nineties, Andy Ghertner was the big dog—and the biggest personality—at Cushman & Wakefield. He trained many brokers and helped them become rising stars in the business. More than anyone else, Andy was the person at the office who gave me hope. At the time, he didn't even know that's what he was doing. Because he was a big dog, doing huge deals with AT&T, Exxon, and all the rest, Andy was one of a few people who had a speaker box on his desk—the sort of contraption where if somebody called you on the phone, you could just press the button on the box and have a conversation with them while you went about other business. As I walked past his office one afternoon, I saw Andy standing on an apple crate with his arms straight out to his sides, his tailor measuring him for a new suit.

To me, it was like a scene out of a Wall Street movie. Andy was talking through his schedule. "No, I won't be able to do that. I'll be fly-fishing with a client." The voice on the other end of the phone proposed another day. "No, I'm taking a client to the Masters that day." And then another: "No, that's the Super Bowl."

I thought, "One day, that's going to be me."

It helped that Andy was also one of the few people who would speak to me on the regular. Other people spoke to me when they needed something from me, but Andy spent time getting to know me and letting me know that he saw something in me. Andy gave me the most important thing you can give anybody in my position:

he let me believe that I could do just what he was doing. With Andy, impossibilities turned into possibilities. He didn't tell me to set my sights a little lower. To the contrary, he was more like "Why not?"

I was driving my daughter to nursery school at seven thirty in the morning when my car phone rang.

"Dallas! Hey, man, this is John."

"John who?"

"John Shlesinger." John was one of Cushman's top brokers in the Atlanta market. Still is, but now with CBRE.

"Hey, John, how're you doing?"

"Where are you, Dallas?"

"I'm taking my daughter to school and then heading to the office."

"I need to talk to you when you get here."

"Okay." I hung up. We had barely talked at all during the three years I'd worked for Cushman & Wakefield. I got my daughter safely to school before the car phone rang a second time.

"Dallas, where are you?"

"I am dropping my daughter off." I grew even more curious about what could possibly be going on that was so urgent. As I pulled into the parking garage, the phone rang a third time.

"John. I am parking. I am coming up now."

By the time I entered the building, John was gesticulating wildly in my direction "Come, come on in!"

John and his partner, Sam Holmes, now both vice chairmen at CBRE and the two biggest tenant representatives in Atlanta (arguably two of the top ten tenant representatives in the entire US), looked suspiciously eager as I entered the room and John closed the door behind me.

"What's going on?"

"Sit down. Do you know Cecil Phillips?"

"No."

"Well, Cecil Phillips has been appointed by the governor to the Georgia Lottery task force."

"Okay."

"We had dinner with him last night, and he thinks the governor is going to get the lottery passed this session. If that happens, they are going to need space, and it's gonna be a good-sized deal—fifty thousand or one hundred thousand square feet plus."

At this point my hearing went away, and I was focused on John's hand gestures. He looked like he was juggling. Sam was sitting next to me on the couch, to my right. John was standing right in front of me, also in front of his desk, waving his hands to convey the enormity of the deal. That's when he said, "We need color on the deal," and pointed to the skin on his arm.

"We need color on the deal."

And then my hearing came back.

For a moment, there was silence. They didn't know if I was offended. But I leaned forward slowly and pointed at my own skin. "Do you know how many deals this has kept me out of? If this can get me in a deal, where do I sign?"

John started laughing.

I'd later come to understand that the reason for "needing color" on the lottery deal was its public-private nature. That, and the man who would be signing the lease on behalf of the state was Black. Cecil had recommended to John and Sam that they could help the deal run more smoothly by having somebody Black on their team.

It took thirty days for us to complete that deal, for nearly 125,000 square feet. It won the *Atlanta Business Chronicle*'s leasing deal of the year award, and it was the first million-dollar check I ever saw.

When that happened, a light came on. I wasn't going to get brought in on deals because people liked me, or were good Christians, or thought I did good work or was a good person. They were going to call me when they absolutely, positively needed to call me. If I wanted to make some real money in this business and in this town, I needed to be the dude who was willing to deal in those moments, no apologies about it.

CHAPTER 4

As Only a Black Man Can Do

When I started at Cushman, my very first cold call was to Herman J. Russell, owner of the top Black construction company in the country. My call reached his secretary, so I told her about how I was the first Black broker at Cushman & Wakefield and that I wanted to talk to Mr. Russell to see if there was any way I might be able to help him. I hung up and decided to take a break from making calls—I was shooting for a hundred calls a day at that point—and I thought about how it could take me a year or two to get to talk with Mr. Russell and how I'd just keep calling until I did.

Not more than fifteen minutes after I'd stepped into the break room, Myra paged me over the intercom. "Dallas, you have a call at the switchboard."

"Just send it here to the break room, Myra," I instructed, assuming my wife was calling to tell me which groceries to pick up on my way home.

"Dallas, this is Mr. Russell."

We quickly exchanged pleasantries, and then I admitted, "Mr. Russell, I'm just being honest with you—I am in the break room right now. I called you from my desk, and I had a whole script ready for what I was going to say to you."

He started laughing.

"I am going to tell you straight from my heart. I am the first Black broker here at Cushman & Wakefield. I am from Atlanta, and you've been an icon to me. I don't know how I can help you or what I can do, but I know whatever I do, I need to be tied to you."

He laughed again. "You tell Noel Khalil"—Noel ran the development arm of his business—"that I've told you to call him. He'll meet with you."

And that's how, back in 1989, I started my relationship with Herman J. Russell.

When I met with Noel, I literally bumped into H. Jerome Russell, H. J.'s son, in the hallway and dropped my business card on the floor. Jerome bent down and picked it up. "Hey, man, I am sorry about that." He looked at the card. "Are you at Cushman & Wakefield?"

"Yes."

"*You* at Cushman & Wakefield?"

"Yeah." I smiled.

"Man, I've got a big interest in commercial real estate. We need to get together."

For three years afterward, we got together for a meal once a month. At one point, Jerome said, "Dallas, when I become president of the company, I want you to come over and start a brokerage company for me."

"Okay," I answered, thinking there was no way that H. J. was turning things over to Jerome anytime soon.

Early in that same three-year period, I invited H. J. Russell & Company to present its interior construction work at one of our broker meetings. Herman J. Russell might have had a reputation for excellence well across the nation at that point, but the white guys at Cushman & Wakefield didn't know him. And I wanted to make sure of two things: that H. J. Russell could get some time to show off in front of that group of brokers, and that everyone at Cushman associated me with everything that the Russell companies did.

Right around the time that the lottery deal happened, the front page of the business section of *The Atlanta Journal-Constitution* featured an article about H. J. handing the reins over to Jerome. One of the guys in the office had seen the paper before I had. "Dallas, have you seen your boy?" I was still taking the paper from his hands when the phone rang. It was Jerome.

"Man, you ready to go to work?"

As part of my interview process with H. J. Russell & Company, I was invited to give a presentation to the board of directors and other company leadership. I don't remember my presentation, but I remember that Vernon Jordan was on that board at the time, and I found presenting myself to a corporate legend intimidating. I started my presentation with a distinction between residential and commercial real estate. "In residential, you might be able to close a deal every day. Now, in commercial, you might not be doing a deal every day, but when you do, when the bell from the cash register rings, you're going to hear it across town."

Vernon chuckled, and in my perception of the moment, he looked at me like "Okay, this kid can sell."

My years at H. J. Russell & Company as vice president of the brokerage division were some of the best of my life. Often I worked personally with H. J., and he was just the wisest man in the world about doing business. I'll give you an example. In a debrief with Mr. Russell about the marketplace, I drew his attention to a big BellSouth deal that was about to occur. I knew about the deal because for five of the years I was at Cushman, I'd been knocking on doors at BellSouth trying to get some business—all to no avail. The company doing BellSouth's work was Carter & Associates—the firm that years back had told me they were not ready to hire a Black broker. Tom Gaither was running the real estate department at BellSouth and was the person working up the deal that was about to take place. It was Tom's habit to work closely with Carter & Associates on all his deals.

As I was debriefing H. J. about all this, he called out to his secretary, "Barb, get Duane on the phone." I had no idea who Duane was. Turns out F. Duane Ackerman was CEO of BellSouth.

"Duane, how you doing?"

"Hey, old man, how you doing?"

"I am good. I am good. Hey, so I got a new brokerage division at the company. My man Darrell"—H. J. had mistakenly called me Darrell once and then decided to stick with his mistake—"tells me you got some nice stuff going down over there, and, you know, I want to get together and see how that fits with what we're doing over here."

"Yeah, let's do it. Tell me when you want to do it."

"How does Monday look?" It was Friday.

"Yeah, okay. We'll make it happen."

H. J. brought a group of us VPs to the meeting, and Duane Ackerman had gathered every president of every division into that room—some of them had to fly in from other cities to attend. It was like *Coming to America* in that room.

The lowest-ranking dude at the table on the BellSouth team was Tom Gaither. Ackerman was at the head of the table with H. J. sitting immediately to his right.

H. J. spoke first. "I want to thank you for putting us together—"

Duane interrupted, "Hold on a minute, H. J. My secretary's out sick today, and I don't want to miss a thing. I want to make sure we take copious notes." He looked down the length of the table to see who might take on that task. "Tom, you take notes." Tom turned red as a beet.

That made my day.

Then Duane turned to me. "Dallas, I'd like to hear from you."

I started telling our story.

"Hold on, hold on," Duane interrupted. "Tom, Tom, do we still have eighty thousand square feet in Birmingham?"

"Yes, we do."

"Give that to Dallas. Do we still have forty thousand square feet in Miami?"

"Yeah."

"Give that to Dallas."

I'd been chasing these dudes at BellSouth for five years, and H. J. had made one call, gathered all the important people into a room in two days' time, and facilitated a bunch of new business for me. I left that one meeting with 120,000 square feet of real estate and scheduled quarterly meetings with the head of BellSouth's real estate planning group.

Herman J. Russell was that dude.

During the time that I was at Cushman & Wakefield, I was also doing comedy at night at different venues in town. I'd even arranged some corporate gigs. But I didn't let the folks at Cushman know about that because I didn't want to be the funny Black guy at the office around all those white people. I really didn't want to be that guy. So I kept those two worlds completely separate from one another. There was Dallas the broker, and there was Dallas the comedian, each in his own silo.

Comedian Dallas was birthed out of the church. I'd always been a bit of a clown, particularly in elementary school. And as a small, skinny kid with a king's nose, I had learned how to defend myself with my words. I was a little guy who could make a bully sit down, and that was pretty powerful. I was also willing to be the mouthpiece for others. I was the guy who would go and ask the teacher, "Is it possible to get ten more minutes of recess? Here's why we need it …" If some guy liked some girl, I'd help him out. "Hey, Jennifer, you know Greg thinks you're really pretty …"

> And as a small, skinny kid with a king's nose, I had learned how to defend myself with my words.

But it wasn't until I was twenty-five years old that I had the epiphany that started my comedy "career." It was June 2, 1987, and I was driving from Charlotte, North Carolina, back to Atlanta after visiting my girlfriend, who would later become my first wife. At the time, it seemed like everyone around me was getting saved and joining the church—including my girlfriend and several of my close guy friends. It was honestly a little lonely when they all made that transition.

On my way through one of the little towns along the route back to Atlanta, I couldn't get a signal on the car radio. When I finally landed on a strong signal, it was a woman's voice—Dr. Daisy, to be exact—that started speaking to me as if she knew me. "You're going here and there, to and fro, and all you're doing is chasing these girls.

You've got this girl over here; you've got this girl over there. You're not putting in your time at school …"

I felt like everything she was saying described me.

"What you're really looking for is agape love. You're looking for unconditional love, and you can only get that from one person. That is the love of Jesus Christ. If you raise your hand now and say the sinner's prayer …"

I was driving, but I closed my eyes, raised my hand, and felt physically and mentally transformed. I was working for Mr. Tift at that time and hadn't taken the day off to make the drive, so I drove right to the office and enthusiastically announced to everyone there, "Hey, I just got saved!" No one was sure how to respond.

A couple of days later, I was listening to the radio again, this time a moving sermon by a Bishop Flynn Johnson—who, it turned out, was a bishop at Atlanta Metropolitan Cathedral. I'd gotten saved on the radio, then two days later I heard Bishop Johnson on the radio, so I decided to go down to his church. When I was there, the pastor asked, "Does anybody want to come up and give testimony?"

I very much did.

So I got up and gave my testimony about how I got saved by Dr. Daisy while driving. I was dead serious, but the audience was cracking up—I mean crying laughing. I went on, "I got saved on the radio; I heard from this church on the radio, now I come here, and this church is in a gym. You've got these basketball hoops. I play basketball. I just know I'm supposed to be here."

After I finished, the pastor came up to me and asked, "Hey, Dallas. Would you like to be the emcee for an annual event we have coming up? You'd just have to talk with the audience and keep the show moving. What do you think?"

And so began my comedy career. I'd do church events, corporate events, even some stand-up. My buddy Jerry and I would do a bit called Pedro and Wallace, based on my father and my Uncle Willard swapping outrageous stories about their youth.

Through the church, I got involved in running camp programs for youth in an organization called Young Life. Each year, we'd have three hundred to four hundred inner-city kids come out to the camp. We'd offer them mentorship and entertainment and encourage them to give their lives over to God.

Harold Milton was an Atlanta lawyer who came out each year to help at the camp. I knew him as the lawyer who came out to help, and he knew me as the comedian who ran programs at the camp. At least, that's how we knew one another until the day when I was called in as "color" to the big meeting to close on the Georgia Lottery deal.

There were easily fifteen people in the conference room at Cushman getting ready for the guy from the state to come in and sign that lease. I was sitting at the end of one side of the table, and the state representative was going to be seated at the opposite head.

When the man from the state arrived, I didn't have my glasses on and was so far down the table that all I saw was just what we were anticipating: the man representing the state was Black. And then I heard that Black man say, "Is that Dallas Smith?"

It was Harold Milton. "Man, that guy is so funny!"

My boss, Mike Elting, looked over at me, then back at Harold. "You mean Dallas?"

I had succeeded at not being the funny Black guy at work. But I had missed the opportunity to know what Harold and I had in common. We'd been around one another for at least five years, but I hadn't known that he was a lawyer for the state, and he had no idea I worked in commercial real estate.

Later, when I was working for H. J. Russell, one of the managers, Paulette Baker, approached me one afternoon. "You didn't tell me you were a comedian!"

"What are you talking about, Paulette?"

"A little bird told me you used to be a comedian. And Dallas, you're going to do it again! I need you to step in and be the entertainment at one of our department events."

"Paulette, I am an officer in this company, and there is no way in hell I'm going to do that."

"None of the people in the audience are people you work with every day. You're going to do it!"

I switched tactics. "Paulette, I get paid to make people laugh. Jerome will have to pay me."

We walked next door to Jerome's office, and Paulette told him what she had in mind. Jerome looked over at me. "Man, I don't even know if you're funny!"

My perspective on the matter changed. "Okay, if I am funny, you pay me fifteen hundred dollars for fifteen minutes. If I'm not funny, you don't have to pay me."

I won't go into detail, except to say that I did a comedy routine for that management group every year for five years straight. At that first event, a lady sitting close to the stage peed herself from laughing so hard.

"That's my endorsement right there," I told Jerome when it came time to collect my $1,500.

As H. J. got closer to retirement, he brought in a new CEO, R. K. Sehgal. From day one, R. K. and I were like oil and water. Not long after he joined the company, I approached Mr. Russell. "I want to start my own company, but I want to continue doing work for you personally." I think H. J. had always thought that I should be working only for him anyway, so he accepted my proposal.

Honestly, by then—this was 2001—I'd grown tired and disenchanted with work, like "nothing to see and do here in Atlanta." So I referred all my clients to a friend and took the year off.

My good friend Daniel Meachum had just become the lawyer for Brian Jordan, who had been a safety for the Atlanta Falcons, then played baseball for the Cardinals, the Braves, the Dodgers, the Rangers, and then the Braves again. At the time I met him, he was playing for the Braves and then moved over to the Dodgers. Danny invited me to one of their meetings because Brian was trying to buy some land. I agreed to sit in on it as a favor to Danny, but I was in the middle of doing other things, so I showed up for the meeting in jeans, a T-shirt, and a ball cap. Danny and Brian were sitting there with BJ's finance guy on the conference line and a real estate guy from a residential firm with them at the table. I knew this real estate guy worked in residential because commercial people don't wear photo ID name tags. This guy was suited and booted, with his fancy pen and his glossy photos of the land. When I came into the room, they were already talking about the deal—three hundred acres or something like that. Danny looked at me after a few minutes and said, "Dallas, you got anything to add?"

"Sure. Have you done an environmental assessment?"

Residential salesman dude looked like a deer in headlights. And then he said some stupid shit. "Dallas, if you really knew this business, you'd know that land is the easiest property to buy."

I was feeling a little bit feisty, so I answered, "*Au contraire, mon frère*. Land is the most difficult thing to buy because you don't know what the fuck you're buying until you do all your due diligence. You need a boundary survey; you need an archaeological survey to let you know what you can tear down and what you can't tear down; you need to know how zoning is going to impact any development you're thinking of doing." Needless to say, I blew up the deal.

BJ was going to spend $2 million, so you can imagine how that residential real estate dude was ready to kill me.

A couple of weeks later, I saw BJ at one of Danny's company parties. "Dallas. Good to see you. What you all doing?"

"We're trying to figure out what we're going to do for Dallas's birthday," Danny answered.

"Why don't you come out to Los Angeles, man? We've got a game coming up this weekend. You can all come to the game, and we can hang out. And I gotta come right back to Atlanta afterward, so you can just come back with me on my plane."

Sounded like a good birthday to me.

We sat right behind the umpire at the Dodgers game. Danny was doing some work for Denzel Washington at the time, so then we went out to Denzel's house and hung out for a bit on his property, talking about filmmaking and ideas. At night, we went to a club called White Lotus. The staff at White Lotus moved Demi Moore, Ashton Kutcher, and Paris Hilton out of the way for the little group of us to sit. Everyone in the club was fawning over Denzel and sizing up me and Danny like, Maybe they're somebody too?

Denzel told the waitress that it was my birthday, and the next thing that happened was that the DJ shouted out, "Oh, we've got Denzel Washington in the house tonight, and one of his boys, it's his birthday. Dallas Smith from Atlanta, this song for you." The song was "Get Low." Two white girls came over to where we were and started hugging me, kissing me, but I knew they were really trying to get over to Denzel. I was just bait along the way, and I was good with that.

We traveled home the next day on Brian's plane—a Citation X—which got us from LA to Atlanta in two and a half hours. I was still in my year of chilling, but BJ decided he was looking to invest in some real estate. We were playing a card game called pluck and just talking casually, but I was also telling him where everyone was building and where I thought would be the next hot area in Atlanta.

We landed. Brian's limo picked us up and took us home. The next morning, Brian called me. "Hey, what's up, man? Let's go look at that property."

"What property?"

"Man, the property you were talking about yesterday. Let's go look at it."

I thought, I was just talking Hollywood shit, man. "Your people call my people" kinda shit. I wasn't having a serious conversation about real estate.

BJ and Danny came over to my house and insisted that we drive around and look at properties. Every property we saw, BJ kept saying he was gonna buy.

"Come on, man. You don't just buy everything you see. You need to put a strategy together."

And that's how we started the development company with his initials as its name. I used a strategy that I learned from Herman J. Russell to help out BJ: buy small, then buy small again—an accumulative process rather than a big thing or a bunch of big things all at once. H. J. had started with one small thing—a single seed—and developed that into a hundred different companies. He wasn't trying to plant the tree from the top down.

The first properties we bought were twenty-six condo units in downtown Atlanta. We took it from 0 to 90 percent leased in a short period of time. But BJ was a $40 million ball player, and a $2 million asset was all too slow for him.

So we ended up doing a larger development, eleven hundred acres in South Fulton with a plan for a thousand homes. Brian, Danny, Erwin Matthews, Steve Macauley, and I were in on the deal. Steve was the first white residential mass developer to work on a project on Atlanta's south side. It was a helluva development, but the timing was wrong—we were about five years too late. The housing bubble of 2006–2007 came along and killed the market. That was a hard pill to swallow. But a great thing came out of that process: I met the young man who would inspire me to uncover my true calling in this business.

For his work on our project, BJ had been given a Developer of the Year award by the Empire Board of Realtists, the oldest Black professional real estate trade association in the US. At the reception, a Morehouse sophomore named Leonte Benton approached BJ to talk about his desire to get into commercial real estate. BJ told him, "I hit baseballs for a living, but if you want to talk real estate, you need to talk to Dallas Smith. He runs that part of the business for me." BJ told Leonte to come by my office for an interview.

I wasn't interested. When he came by the office, I mispronounced his name. Honestly, it didn't matter to me what his name was because I fully expected never to see him again. "Do you have a real estate license, Leo-teen?"

"No, sir."

"Well, go get your license, and we'll talk."

By that point, I'd said those same words to at least fifty people over the years, and nobody ever came back. When I left Mr. Russell, I had no permanent office. I would work the first quarter of the year, then take the rest of the year off. I didn't have responsibility for any brokers. I wasn't paying for extra office space. I didn't have to buy desks, pay for phones, or train a team.

In a sense, I was still living like it was all about me. I wasn't developing business long term. I was just trying to put money in my pocket.

When I told Leonte to go get his license, I fully expected that I wouldn't ever see him again. But in three weeks' time, he was back. "Mr. Smith. I've got my license." I couldn't even remember who he was. I never had plan B because plan A—get rid of people—always worked.

Now I was thinking, Damn. What am I going to do with this kid?

I told him to come into the office every day. And he did. For two whole weeks. I had him wash my car, get me coffee, run my clothes to and from the cleaner's, get my dog from the kennel. I had him doing all kinds of stupid stuff, hoping he'd eventually say, "You know what, man? Fuck you!" and just get the hell out. But he never did. He did everything I asked with a smile, always very pleasant and very unassuming.

One day UPS delivered some water to the office, and I asked Leonte, "Can you put the water away for me?"

"Yes, sir."

He knelt down in a full suit and tie and started putting the water into the cabinet. Looking at him so dutifully doing what I'd asked, I had an epiphany from God.

Dallas, that was you. That was you when you were trying to get into the commercial real estate business, and there was nobody who looked like you who could help you. You could help this kid, unlike anybody was ever able to help you.

It was at that moment that I knew why I'd gone through every single minute of my life. It was my duty to develop a company of people who looked like me, to help them get established in the industry and excel.

> **It was my duty to develop a company of people who looked like me.**

That epiphany took place at the same time that the company I'd invested in with BJ was falling off a cliff.

I didn't say anything to Leonte until later that day, when I called him with instructions. "Meet me at the Ritz-Carlton downtown."

We sat together at a small table. "Leonte, let me tell you something. The company I'm part of is about to implode. I'm gonna start my own company. BJ introduced me to you, so if you want to roll with him, I understand. But if you want to roll with me—"

Before I could finish my sentence, Leonte blurted out, "I am rolling with you, Mr. Smith!"

"Okay then. It looks like we are starting a company."

Leonte and I shook hands, and T. Dallas Smith & Company was born. That was December 2006, and we officially became a company in March 2007. I told Leonte, "Give me five years of your time. I am going to teach you this business from top to bottom. I guarantee you that by the time you get out of college, you will be making more money than all of your friends. Money is the last thing you'll be worried about."

In all honesty, that hadn't been the case for me. I was the guy who made $300,000 and spent $600,000; I made $600,000, and I spent $1 million. That was a habit I'd "learned" from Mr. Tift when the true differences between him and me hadn't been entirely clear in my mind. Mr. Tift could always fall back on his inheritance, whereas I had nothing to fall back on.

CHAPTER 5

Service First

Though I might have been a young man when I got started in the commercial real estate business, I also started out with an ego that was completely out of whack. I've half-jokingly blamed Dr. Schwartz for helping to stoke that ego, but I developed it a bit earlier than when I met him, around the time when I discovered that dressing well and having a nice car at Tennessee State would attract the ladies. That said, hearing for years from the man who wrote *The Magic of Thinking Big* that there was "just nobody better than Smith" was something that my young mind didn't quite know how to handle or accept with humility. I'd always suspected that I was a person who was going to do great things, and then Schwartz went and confirmed it. Out loud. To everyone.

At Cushman & Wakefield, it was as if all the egomaniacs had gathered together in a single place. The Rockefeller family owned that business, and there was an unspoken rule that they only hired people who came from money. That environment ended up tempering my ego a bit—just being around so many people who grew up having mansions and planes and yachts. I certainly gained some perspective from having that experience. That said, I had also gotten into the business precisely because I had set "make a lot of money" as my primary goal.

It was early on in my time at Cushman & Wakefield that I took that second job keying in car tags at the airport—the job I'd settled on when my father had wanted me to work at the post office instead. One of those evenings at the airport, I caught sight of my boss, Mike Elting, walking directly toward me. Worried that he would recognize me and unsure what to do about that, I ended up standing there frozen in place. Even more than I didn't want to be the funny Black guy at the office, I didn't want anyone there to know that I was keying tags in the evenings. The business was opposed to its brokers working part-time jobs, and I didn't need my boss catching me at this particular part-time gig.

I need not have worried. Mike walked right past me, and in that moment, I felt completely invisible. I suppose I might have been glad that I hadn't been found out, but instead I thought about how I was working as the type of service person that no one paid attention to. My boss had passed me by just as if I'd been a nondescript piece of furniture. I could not imagine tolerating having that experience day after day.

It was around that time when I started going out of my way to take better care of the way I treated the people around me every day. I'd had plenty of experience wanting to be seen and acknowledged by others—and a good dose of enjoyment from being seen and appreciated—and I wanted to be sure I never made others feel less than or invisible around me.

People I would see day to day—those who guarded or cleaned the building or staffed its front desk—always got some attention from me.

In them, I saw myself—the person who was invisible while checking airport tags, but also the person who was aware that if certain things hadn't worked out at critical points along the way, I could very easily have found myself doing that for a living.

I've seen a lot of people, especially men, wholesale discount the people who work in service-oriented jobs. You probably know the sort of person I'm talking about—someone who shows up to Eddie Somebody-or-other's office and nearly shouts at the secretary, "Tell Eddie I'm here!" My dude, how about "Hello. Good morning. How are you doing?" possibly followed by "I'm here to see Eddie; is he available?"

Not bothering to greet people as people is so disrespectful. In trying to do just the opposite, I remembered how my parents raised me. My dad had that special ability to befriend everyone from the lowest person cleaning the building to the CEO. I'd always admired that about my dad and

The thing is, it's really very easy to be kind.

often explicitly prayed, "Lord, let me have some of that."

The thing is, it's really very easy to be kind. The main security guard in my current office building loves lemon tea. So every time I come in and she's there, I check to see if she needs some.

"You have your tea?"

"Yeah, I have my tea."

When I go by and she doesn't, I'll come back up to our office, make the tea, and bring it down to her.

It's a simple gesture. If I were sitting in her seat, and I'd been there all day, I'd have at least one expectation of anyone who came by: speak to me—directly to me. If I were in that role, I'd appreciate if someone said, "Good morning, Dallas." Now if that person also said, "How're you doing?" and listened for my honest answer, that'd be wonderful. And if that person also said, "Hey, you want some of that tea you like?"—well, that would be a whole 'nother level. That person might become my best guy.

Myra did that for me all the times I visited Cushman & Wakefield interviewing for a job. And then she went out of her way for me when she introduced me to Bill Bugg.

While I'd been good about taking care with people, the one not-so-good thing I continued to do until I was in my midforties was focus on the money—on earning as much of it as I possibly could.

The first moment I recognized that I was mistaken to focus primarily on money was when Danny and BJ invited me out to California and we spent time at Denzel's house on my birthday. We were walking in the garden and stopped at a plaque engraved with the famous Eleanor Roosevelt quote "Great minds discuss ideas; average minds discuss events; small minds discuss people." Denzel stopped and tapped my arm with the back of his hand. "That's what we need to do. We need to get together from time to time just to talk about ideas."

Talking about ideas is one part figuring things out or pinning them down, another part recognizing just how much things are always evolving. It's also no parts chasing money. What resonated with me for the first time that afternoon was that if you're chasing money, you're chasing the wrong thing. So many people get stuck chasing money and then can't get out of their own way; they'll even see obstacles where there aren't any. If the first thing you think when you have an idea is "I don't have the money to do that," you're missing out on the opportunity to think things through or find unique solutions to a problem you're trying to solve. More and more, I've come to think the reality is that you don't need the money; there are workarounds when it comes to the actual money. What you need are people to help you go through the thought processes that allow you to figure out what's really possible.

The more friends I make who aren't bound by concerns about money, the more I notice that they approach questions and problems without the expectation that there will be any limitations on what they can do. They make a plan, they move forward, and they work around whatever comes up. If a limit presents itself, the question is "Okay, how do we get over this?" It's always "Let's get over this" and never "We can't."

When we started T. Dallas Smith & Company, we had no money and no clients. It was me and Leonte, a service-hearted guy with no real estate experience. We didn't draw up a business plan, but even if I'd written something down on paper to present to investors, it wouldn't have looked promising. Imagine it:

"I'd love for you to invest in my company."

"Okay, Dallas. What is your company?"

"Well, I'm going to do commercial real estate, representing companies that want to rent or buy properties."

"Oh, okay. Who's going to be helping you?"

"This young man here, who I'm going to train."

"All right. How much capital do you have?"

"Well, we don't have any money. I'm living off my sister's credit card right now. And you know, you take from Peter to pay Paul. But I know we're going to get through it."

Nobody would ever have invested in that. But I knew without a doubt this thing was going to work. I didn't have money—wrecked, as

I'd been, by the markets crashing in 2006 and 2007—but I did have an idea. Since everything that we would need to start up a full-service real estate company cost money that we didn't have—even little things like putting up a sign or setting up a website—that forced me to focus the business only on tenant representation. I didn't need a sign or a site to get that started.

If I'd had all the money in the world, I probably would have done what everybody else was already doing. Instead, when I started my own business, there was nobody else in town who looked like us, nobody with anything but a full-service firm. That was our differentiator at the start, and to this day, that's still what we do. I don't think anyone ever really feels grateful to be broke, but I will acknowledge that being broke was the catalyst for establishing our niche. We couldn't afford to do more, so we didn't. We found a way to get over the limit that presented itself.

Right after I talked with Leonte about my idea and began seriously preparing to start my own company, I met with Andy Ghertner for lunch.

"I'm going to start my own company. What do you think?"

"What took you so long?" Andy added, "You know I'm Jewish. I understand how this works. Blacks have got to do the same thing. You need to do the same things I did."

"Well, Andy, let me ask you for a favor. Would you agree to be on my 'unofficial' board of directors?"

"Absolutely."

I rented space for me and Leonte in a WeWork environment, and that's where we met Kellie Agno, who worked for a company situated opposite ours. She'd approached us to talk about her interest in commercial real estate and then kept coming by, inquiring about opportunities to work with us. She dropped in one Friday afternoon, still eager to learn, so I offered her a thirty-second, bare-minimum education.

"Here's a letter of authorization. This is how we get hired. If you can get one of these signed, we can have a conversation."

I should have learned from Leonte that some people were not going to be deterred by my disinterest. But I was once again genuinely surprised when Kellie came back early on Monday, announced, "I could only get three," and handed me three signed LOAs.

What I said to Kellie was "Let me look at these, and we'll talk." But what I thought was What in the hell!

We'd brought on a few other brokers by that point, and altogether they hadn't managed to serve up what Kellie had—and she'd done it without any real knowledge of the field and in fewer than thirty-six hours from the "lesson" I'd offered.

I called my cousin Eric. "Eric. Help me understand this, man. She's got three deals that she did over the weekend."

Eric offered sage advice. "Dallas, if I had to choose between hiring your ugly ass or hiring a beautiful woman, I'm gonna hire the beautiful woman every time."

Kellie was a beast of a salesperson. She would show up at a conference or seminar and come back with deals. Here in Atlanta, she brought two other brokers with her to an event they were not registered to attend. Kellie took three name tags off the table and told her colleagues, "Just follow me." She introduced herself to someone and locked him in as a client, then the three of them put back the name tags and left the event. That woman could cold call a potential client with a reputation as a hard-ass and walk out of his office with a deal in hand.

That was Kellie. Not long after she started working with us, she ended up moving back to Hawaii to be near family. But she's still technically on our roster because whenever Kellie decides that she's ready to work again, we will be more than ready to welcome her back!

It was Leonte, Kellie, and me who met with Andy Ghertner for four hours of initial business planning. I will always give credit to Andy for being that guy. He was willing to offer help and then take the time to give that help. We learned some of his secrets for building his brand, and sometimes we were surprised by his answers to our questions.

"Andy, did you have a financial goal every year that you wanted to meet?"

"Nope."

We heard stories of how he hung out at the Capital City Club every Monday and Wednesday—sometimes meeting with clients, sometimes just being present there so that people would come to know and recognize him. Tuesdays and Thursdays he'd do the same thing somewhere else, at a restaurant that was also a prime gathering spot for the clientele he wanted to attract. He was at these places so much that people thought he owned them.

It's my style to learn through mimicry, so after hearing that story, Leonte and I generated a list of "activity goals"—high-touch practices like frequenting a set of restaurants and giving generous tips to the valets. Then, no matter what we were doing there or what we were driving—and, let me say, Leonte had a pretty beat-up car at the time—those guys would park us right up front, and we'd enjoy excellent service once inside. True to form, people would take notice. When you're waiting twenty minutes for your Bentley and Leonte's beat-up Camry is parked right up front, you're going to notice.

Andy also displayed quiet signs of wealth in the way he dressed— the fold of his pocket square, the style of braces he wore with suits, his choice of belts. I've mentioned his personal tailor, but he'd also accumulated a host of completely understated and very expensive accessories. They were of the sort you'd recognize only if you already knew the brand and its value (and exactly the opposite of expensive brands that flaunt their names and logos all over their products). I started copying these details from Andy's wardrobe, sometimes down to the exact items he owned.

Given the caliber of clients that Andy attracted, following his lead continued to give me hope, even when we couldn't afford a lick of what we were doing. He helped me see that starting up on my own was possible. Andy had been the first Jewish commercial broker in the area to compete with all the white Anglo-Saxon Protestant males. He understood the challenges and the pain that came with my effort to be among the first Black men to do the same; he'd had to deal with those challenges and that pain too.

Andy didn't cower in the face of pain, and he also didn't pretend he could ignore it. Instead, he used it. He stood up and said, "Okay, why not me?" And that's exactly the gift he gave to me: the hope to also ask, "Why not me too?" I'd studied him, talked with him, and concluded, Okay, I might have to do more work than he did, but if I follow the same path as that guy, I, too, might succeed.

Andy helped us get clear on our purpose and plan for T. Dallas Smith & Company. My sister let me use her credit cards until I was able to earn enough to pay her back. Having two sisters who had faith in me and loved me dearly, and one who was willing to let me run her credit into the ground, made a world of difference in those early days. So did the consistent support of my new wife, Monica. Monica met me when I had lots of money; then I lost lots of money, and still she stuck with me. She could have bounced, but she was able to see the journey that I was on, and she chose to stand with me.

After a while, I was able to acquire some office space downtown, but everything was still a struggle. At one point, I could pay the office rent but not the mortgage on our house. I'd been at the office every day that week and, in anticipation of having to move, had been repeatedly checking on a condo complex where there were never any availabilities. On the weekend, I took our dog out in the yard and started talking to God. "You've got me out here doing this thing. But it's just not working. I can't pay both the office rent and our mortgage."

Clear as clear can be, I heard the reply: "You can get another house."

I headed back inside, already expecting that it could take weeks to convince Monica that it was a good idea to move and half expecting that she might not speak to me in the interim.

"Monica, I was just out talking to God. I can't pay both the mortgage and the office rent. God said, 'You can get another house.' Are you okay with walking away from this house?"

"Okay."

It was that easy. If her reply wasn't a confirmation from God, I don't know what would have been.

I thought about the condo complex and how God's message that afternoon hadn't ended with permission to sell the house. God had also said about the condo complex, "Just go down there."

So I did.

I stated my interest to the concierge on duty. "How funny." She smiled. "There's someone moving out this afternoon." She introduced us, and just like that, I'd found the right place for our family to live.

There's a bit of scripture in Psalms 37:23 that reads, "The footsteps of a righteous man are ordered by the Lord." I've thought a lot about how my steps have guided me to the person or the situation I needed at just the moment I needed them. I'd bumped into Jerome Russell and dropped my business cards at his feet. I walked into that condo complex as a tenant was moving out. And soon after that, I would meet one of my prized business partners when he bumped into my chair at a local event.

Five years into the business, Dexter, Leonte, and I went out to San Francisco to have dinner with Cort Bishop, director of real estate transactions for AT&T. Cort was a white guy from the West Coast with a real heart for diversity and was thoroughly disgruntled with how efforts toward equality were coming along in the US. Years before we showed up to meet with him, Cort had been asking all the big shot firms, "Where's your diversity?"

I remember looking over at Leonte on the plane ride, floored by the difference between my career and his. "Leonte, it's taken me twenty-eight years to have this dinner, and it's only taken you five."

We'd gotten connected with Cort through Al Taylor, a Black senior manager of AT&T's real estate portfolio and a man to whom we owe a debt of gratitude for what he planted with that introduction. Al had introduced us to Karlos McGhee, and both Al and Karlos helped us through the process of getting access to Cort.

Dinner was excellent, because Cort always picked the best restaurants and then made sure everyone enjoyed the best wines and the best food. His first move was to see about getting us to work along with some of these other firms. But those firms didn't want to work with us. That's what led Cort to find us something to work on ourselves. He gave us our own contract—and that was a game changer.

Our work with Cort led to multiple big transactions. Nevertheless, it took seven years of deals with AT&T before that company's Diversity, Equity, and Inclusion office found out about us. When they did, they reached out with all these forms they wanted filled out just for us to be officially registered with them. My sense of a lot of DEI initiatives in white-run businesses is that those initiatives end up being run by people who look like me and who don't have the clout or the power to push through an agenda that would make a difference. From what I've seen, one week you've got a broom closet, and the next, it's the new DEI office. Put a white man with the ear of the CEO in that position, and maybe something good will come out of it. Until that happens, I'm going to insist on walking through the front door and dealing with the people who do have the power to make meaningful change.

At one of our dinners years later, we gave Cort a little award—an ink pen monogrammed with the number forty-two. It was 2013, and the movie *42*, tracking the story of Jackie Robinson's rise as the first African American player in modern Major League Baseball, had just been released. We'd given Cort this particular gift because we wanted to honor him for being our Branch Rickey, the owner of the Brooklyn Dodgers who put Jackie Robinson in the game and gave him an opportunity. We even called it the "Branch Rickey Award." Cort Bishop was that guy, a white man with a heart for helping to change the narrative in a white-dominated industry.

Later that same year, I got a call from John O'Neill, who was then running Cushman & Wakefield's Atlanta office and has since then become that company's president of US Multifamily Capital Markets. At the time, John was about to become the president of the Atlanta Commercial Board of REALTORS and wanted to do some programming around diversity during his tenure in the role. Of course, he called the Black guy in the business to ask for help.

"I really want to do something around diversity, Dallas."

"Okay." I was holding the phone, thinking, Man, I've been hearing this for years now, and I've seen how these programs are aimed more at optics than any real and lasting change.

"I want to know if you'll help me."

"Okay, John. Do me a favor. Go see the movie *42*, and then give me a call."

A week later he called back.

"Have you seen the movie, John?"

"No. Not yet."

"John, see the movie, and then we'll talk."

A couple days more and he'd seen the movie.

"All right. Tell me your takeaways."

"Jackie went through a whole lot."

"Yeah. What else?"

John offered a couple more insights, all of them focused on Jackie.

Eventually I interrupted. "John, the reason I wanted you to see the movie is because I want you to understand one thing. People talk like Jackie Robinson just put on a uniform, walked out on the field, and started playing baseball. That's not what happened. A white man named Branch Rickey decided that he was going to integrate baseball. He knew that it was white men holding the keys, keeping Black men locked out of the game, and it was his decision to act in a way that would change that. Then he got KKK crosses burned in his yard. He got threatened with being kicked out of his country club. His friends stopped talking to him. He dealt with a lot of stuff that white men did not have to deal with. He put his toe in my pond. Unless you're willing to do that, John, lose my number."

"Well, Dallas, they're either gonna come along with us or not." He paused. "And if they don't, fuck 'em." At that point I knew that John was my guy.

Together, we formulated a four-point plan to attack two big influences on the lack of diversity in the commercial real estate business: racism and a lack of exposure. Black people didn't have enough models to make them aware that this career path even existed. And they didn't have those models because white people kept shutting Black people out of the business.

Up until the early 1960s, two things were true: First, the National Association of Realtors didn't allow Black people to become Realtors (there was an alternative association called the National Association of Real Estate Brokers, whose members were named Realtists and who served the needs of the Black community). And second, white Realtors were restricted from selling homes in white areas to Black people. Even the Fair Housing Act of 1968 didn't change much; it wasn't until the mid-1970s that the National Association of Realtors formally affirmed a nondiscrimination policy that would "welcome" Blacks into the organization. At the time John contacted me to brainstorm about programs we might facilitate—just as today—there was a separate organization for Black brokers in Atlanta called the Empire Board of Realtists.

With all that in mind, John and I put together our four programs to bring historically Black and white associations into conversation with one another. By 2014, we were fully implementing three of them. The first was annual "fireside chats" that I named Commercial Real Estate Studio (CRE Studio for short) after the television show hosted by James Lipton called *Inside the Actors Studio*. That show, for those who remember, was basically a craft seminar conducted as in-depth interviews with famous actors and actresses. CRE Studio was a means of addressing the concern of exposure to those who've been successful in the industry as an important part of recruiting a more diverse membership. Next, we started a mentor-mentee program for young people interested in the profession to give regular and personalized exposure to those who wanted to know more or were already in training to join the commercial real estate industry. Third, we arranged for the Empire Board of Realtists to have a seat on ACBR's board of directors.

When John and I discussed this, he questioned, "Does the Empire Board even have a commercial real estate division?"

"Yeah, they do."

"Well, who's chair?"

"I'm chair."

"Oh, okay. Well, we should definitely do that."

I got off that call with John and checked in with then Empire Board president Stacey Mollison. "Stacey, don't we have a commercial council at Empire?"

"Yeah, we do, but it's defunct."

"Well, listen, I need you to undefunct it and make me chair."

That's how it came to be that once annually the boards of the Black and white real estate organizations of Atlanta started coming together. It wasn't until two years later that I told John the story of how the commercial council came back into being. Nearly every year since then, one of the brokers at T. Dallas Smith & Company has headed up the commercial group at Empire. And Empire now has a seat at the table along with other affiliate board chairs like Commercial Real Estate Women (CREW) Network, Society of Industrial and Office Realtors (SIOR), and Certified Commercial Investment Member (CCIM) Institute.

For the fourth program in our plan, we envisioned holding an annual two-day race awareness workshop. Within a year, we'd accomplished the first three items, really given those programs a good foundation and set them in motion. That was a helluva lot for one year.

But the race awareness piece stalled. I waited to hear from John about his readiness to move forward.

By 2017, John got back in touch about the workshop. Al Vivian ran the first one in 2018, and we've had another each year since. Getting that inaugural group of thirty together was a lot of work. Let me clarify: it was no work to get eight Black real estate professionals to agree to attend. They were more than happy to participate. But convincing our white colleagues was trickier. Many of them initially responded to John with something like "What the hell? Why are you doing this?"

So we wined and dined them, and made our best case. "If we're gonna make this change, we want you to be in the room. We're all going to look back years from now and be like 'Hey, we did that.'"

I may also have tricked one of them into attending. I'd been asked to speak at a DEI kickoff event at one of the Atlanta brokerages. During the Q&A, someone in the audience asked a big, open-ended question: "How do we deal with the whole race issue?"

"Funny you should ask." I knew exactly what I wanted to say next. "Is Mike Sivewright here? Mike, can you stand up for a minute? John and I are planning a two-day race awareness workshop, and I would love for you"—in front of these one hundred people and these cameras rolling—"to say that you'll be the first one to sign up for it!"

Mike let out a slow "Yeeeaaaaaaah?"

I called John after the event. "You're not gonna believe who I got to sign up!"

That workshop was, and still is, an uncomfortable one for white people because it forces people to undergo the experience of being marginalized just as much as it forces people to look in the mirror at their own marginalizing practices. When we invite participants, we don't describe the event much except to say, "It's something that'll change your life." And it always does, always for the better.

I've been in this business now for over forty years, but I didn't come into my calling until 2006, when Leonte, with his wise and service-oriented heart, patiently did whatever I asked of him as I tried with all my might to get him to leave me alone. That afternoon when he knelt down to unload a case of water, I learned that I was supposed to spend the rest of my life building up Black people in this business so that operating at the highest levels is much easier for them than it ever was for me. People like Andy Ghertner had given me hope that I could succeed; it became my duty to do the same for others.

> People like Andy Ghertner had given me hope that I could succeed; it became my duty to do the same for others.

I was forty-four years old when I learned two important lessons about service: one, that I was supposed to commit myself to bringing up the next generation of Black commercial real estate brokers; and two, that I had always been in a service profession. Brokers, like doctors or lawyers—but also like security guards or secretaries—are facilitators, intermediaries whose work on behalf of clients, if done well, makes the system work so that people can get about the primary business of moving forward with their lives. A good broker, in my opinion, approaches each opportunity guided by the question "How am I going to impact people's lives in a positive way?"

CHAPTER 6

Three Smooth Stones

When Dexter Warrior bumped into my chair, I felt the push of fate.

We were at the Atlanta History Center for the annual dinner of the National Association of Industrial and Office Parks (NAIOP). I was at John Portman's table at Brian Hogg's invitation—me and nine white guys sitting around a ten top. Out of a thousand people at the dinner, there were two Black people: me and Dexter.

As it happened, I was seated on one side of the ballroom, Dexter on the completely other side of the ballroom. I'd just finished talking to somebody at our table and pushed my chair back to stand up. That's when Dexter bumped into me.

I didn't know that Dexter wasn't working with Morgan Stanley anymore, so I asked, "How's Morgan Stanley?"

"Man, that chapter of my life is over. I'm trying to figure out my next thing."

Immediately I said, "I know what you need to do, Dexter. You need to come work with me doing tenant rep." I added, "You've been stealing from tenants your entire career. Everything you've done to hurt them—now you can help them!"

Dexter laughed.

"No, man, I'm serious. I'm being serious."

I knew that my personality needed Dexter's personality as a balance. If I'm always walking around thinking the glass is half-full even when the glass is near emptied, Dexter is the guy who, when the glass is more than three-quarters full, is thinking we're almost out. I've always been a gunslinger kind of a guy, a salesman at heart, and Dexter's a hardwired corporate guy—structured, knowledgeable about the rules, and committed to following them. He'd made his name working pension funds handling billions of dollars in commercial real estate transactions on the landlord side of the business. I knew that if we could bring Dexter's knowledge and experience to bear on the tenant side of the transaction, nobody could mess with us.

Much later on, Dexter would ask me how I knew that we would get along.

"Dude, I've watched you."

I wasn't kidding. We were at Georgia State together when Dexter became the university's first Black Student Government Association president. He ran against some white frat boys. The first time I saw Dexter was on his campaign poster. I looked at that poster, thinking, This dude's got to be crazy. Ain't no way in hell! To be clear, that was Georgia State in the early 1980s when less than 5 percent of the students were Black. When he won, I wondered, Who is this guy? And as I watched him operate, I realized he was extremely buttoned up, the most corporate of corporate guys, and extremely talented.

Thanks to Dr. Schwartz's encouragement, I'd learned the value of selling, and I'd learned that I was good at it. That's how I knew that Dexter Warrior would be the perfect balance to me when it came to making our company whole. I knew there'd be people who wouldn't like me who would absolutely love him and people who wouldn't like him but who would love me.

About a month after that NAIOP dinner, Georgia State University was working on recruiting me to their foundation board. Jerome Russell was supposed to call me to set up a meeting, but he never got to it and said as much at a board meeting. Dexter, who was already on the board, reacted to Jerome's update by offering, "Well, I know Dallas. I can reach out to him myself."

Dexter and Nancy Peterman, who was president of the Georgia State Foundation Board at the time, met up with me for a lunch interview to see if I was a good candidate for appointment. Nancy asked, "Dallas, how was your time at Georgia State?"

"Nancy, do you want the honest answer?"

"Yeah, I want the honest answer."

"It was the most fucked-up situation I ever was in ..."

Dexter turned multiple shades of red.

"... until I met David Schwartz. But until that time ..."

As a student at Georgia State, it had been obvious to me that I wasn't welcome. All but a couple of teachers confirmed my suspicion that no one could imagine what I was doing there.

When Nancy excused herself from the table, I turned to Dexter. "Dex, man, you got a minute? I'd love to walk you over to my office to show you what I'm doing."

AT&T's southeastern coverage area was a nine-state district, and the federal government's southeastern district was eight states. By then, I'd acquired ten state licenses to allow us to work comfortably for both organizations. I'd hung my licenses on one of the big columns in my office, and when Dexter came in, his first word was "Wow."

"Yeah. Dude, I'm serious about this."

"All right. Let me give it some thought."

Dexter had been earning great money with Morgan Stanley; he had benefits and all the certainty and security that comes along with a solid corporate structure. He hadn't done anything entrepreneurial, yet there I was calling, "Come jump on over here, brother. The water's fine, but there's no telling if it will stay that way." I knew it was going to be a hard sell, but I also just felt convinced that it was going to land. I couldn't tell you why. I just knew it was going to land.

As Dexter was leaving the office, I introduced him to Leonte. Once Dexter had gone, Leonte asked, "Who's that?"

"Man, that's Michael Jordan. And he's sitting on the bench. We got to get him in the game."

Not more than a couple of days later, I got a call from Dexter.

"Dallas, I may have our first assignment."

A church member had called on Dexter out of the blue, saying, "My aunt's looking for some real estate. She needs ten to fifteen thousand square feet of real estate. She asked me if I knew anybody who could help her out, and I thought about you."

"Man, Dexter, I know you're a spiritual brother. If you don't see God's handwriting on the wall with this one … I mean, God just handed us the ram in the bush."

We pitched our business, and the woman's aunt hired us. That deal turned into another, and between both we made about $200,000.

The real unsung hero in the story of Dexter coming on board at T. Dallas Smith & Company is Dexter's mother. She did not know me from Adam. But when Dexter told her about the opportunity to work with me, his mother said, "Dexter, let me tell you something about a guy like Dallas. If he succeeded once before, he'll do it again."

The year that we made over $10 million, I asked Dexter if I could be the one to tell his mom. I was almost in tears, and she was most definitely in tears. I told her, "Thank you. It was your vote of confidence in me that got your son to say, 'Well, maybe going along with this guy is not such a bad thing to do.'"

In the commercial real estate business, I think about those of us who work at T. Dallas Smith & Company as the Davids going up against a lot of Goliaths. The way I've always understood that bit of scripture, this scrawny little guy turns out to be the only one who raises his hand to say he'll go and fight a dangerous giant.

> **I think about those of us who work at T. Dallas Smith & Company as the Davids going up against a lot of Goliaths.**

The people in his community, worried that he's got little chance of success, begin to outfit him in armor. But the armor is too heavy to bear. So instead of going to battle loaded down with steel plating, swords, and other weaponry, he goes only with a simple slingshot and three smooth stones. To top it off, David is such a good shot that he only needs to use one of those three stones to land the giant.

David is a young man who seems woefully unprepared for battle, but he's got the courage and the skill to take down a giant. "I've fought the lion and the bear," he announces. "I can take this guy too."

That story comes to mind for me when I'm talking with younger people who are interested in getting into commercial real estate or starting up their own firms. Our little group is always going up against the biggest firms on the planet—the ones with billions of dollars, brokers with years of tenure, and networks of relationships that span multiple lifetimes. We have none of those things. We have no armor; we have no military weaponry. What we have is a small team of brokers and three small stones—our three managing partners: me,

Leonte, and Dexter. But sometimes we land Goliaths smack dab in the middle of their foreheads.

Our work is more than just straight up trying to get business. First, we've got to unseat the giants. We're a small commercial company, the only one full of people who look like we do, and by comparison with others, we're still relatively new on the scene. The reality is that it's easiest for Fortune 500 companies—or Fortune 100 companies, for that matter—to pick their brokers from one of the top three giant firms in the nation. It's a security-oriented move; should something go wrong, those companies can't be faulted for choosing from among the biggest, best, and longest-standing companies. And they can't be faulted for honoring the long-standing relationships they've developed with those firms and with individual brokers representing those firms. Maybe they've hired Johnny to handle their real estate for the past fifteen years. Maybe they go golfing, or fishing, or hunting with Johnny on a regular basis.

That's why we've got to be persistent and pay close attention. Because one day Johnny is going to mess up or let down his guard. And that's when we'll strike.

Let's say Johnny put his client into a building without disclosing that his firm also is doing the leasing on the building. After that happens a couple of times, the client's head of real estate is likely to wonder, Hey, wait a minute, did Johnny really have our interests front and center, or was he just looking to profit off both sides of the transaction?

Or maybe what happens is that Johnny gets lazy. He first pitched the business to his client twenty years ago, when he was hungry and doing all the work himself. Then Johnny brought a couple of people with him on his deals, and now that team has got a much bigger book of business. Johnny's not just doing deals in Georgia anymore; he's working all across the United States. He doesn't show up for every deal anymore, and he only answers the phone when there's a hundred thousand square feet and a million-dollar fee on the table. The people he's got working the other deals are junior brokers because he can pay the junior people less when the fees come in. Now the client who's relied on Johnny for the past twenty years is no longer getting the type of quality that they expected back when Johnny originally pitched the business.

After a while that client's head of real estate might start to think that it's time to reassess their business with Johnny. They want to see if there's something else out there. That's most likely to happen when there's a shake-up within the company's real estate department. A new person comes in, does an assessment of the past few years' deals, and sees that every deal has used the same firm.

Now imagine if that head of real estate puts everything on the line to hire our little firm instead, people he doesn't know as well and who may even seem to him underprepared for the task at hand.

My approach has always been this: when we see a crack, we work on wedging ourselves in. When we get that opportunity, we've got to knock it out of the park, overserve on even the smallest deals—a thousand square feet, five thousand, the sorts of deals where a lot of those other shops won't even bother to pick up the phone. Next thing you know, it's not Goliath but David who has that company's business. But it didn't happen overnight. It was a long process, a lot of time, and often a lot of relationship building before even that first little deal came to pass.

Cort Bishop put everything on the line to hire our little firm. He'd inquired about diversity in the firms AT&T worked with, and the answer had always come back, "There's nobody out there, and we've tried. Lord knows we've looked high and low." Then Cort gave

us an opportunity and became our advocate along with Al Taylor
and later Karlos McGee, Russ McFadden, Orin Odom, and Cherise
Mlott.

At one of those great check-in dinners, Cort brought with him
four stacks of paper and laid them out on the table in front of us. "I
don't understand this" was all he said.

"What are you talking about?" I asked.

"All right, here's the deal …"

Cort explained that one of those stacks of papers was from T.
Dallas Smith & Company; the other three were from the three biggest
brokerage firms on the planet.

"I've looked through these," Cort announced, "and on average,
T. Dallas Smith & Company's net aggregate value"—that's the total
out-of-pocket expense for a lease—"is thirteen percent less than all
the others. How is that possible?"

I set down my wineglass and offered my best off-the-cuff explanation. "Cort. We're not all members of the same country club."

"Huh?"

"Think about it like this. The biggest, the most successful guys
in our business are all members of country clubs where it's likely that
the landlords who own the buildings those brokers are leasing are also
members. If I'm your broker and I'm trying to get your deal done with
one particular landlord who also is a member of the same country club
as me, it's likely we're just going to pull each other over at the bar and
have a conversation like this: 'Jim, I really need to be at fifty dollars a
foot.' 'Man, Todd, I've got to have sixty dollars. I've got to.' Jim and
Todd will order another drink, and then Todd will offer, 'Okay, I'll tell
you what. I can get you to fifty-eight dollars.' They'll toast the deal,
and Jim will return to his client. 'I got you a good deal at fifty-eight
dollars a foot. That's a really good deal.' But the reality of it, Cort?

It's not a good deal. But it is a deal that will sustain Jim and Todd's friendship. So the reason those other firms are on average thirteen percent higher than ours is because there is a hidden friendship tax."

Cort loved that answer. His only response was to laugh out loud and say, "Damn."

Now, I talk a lot about the importance of building relationships, but I can also say that even when the person with whom I'm negotiating is someone I know, even a good friend, I take steps to ensure that our friendship is not going to be an issue during a transaction. I might, for example, insert another broker from my shop into the process—someone who doesn't know the landlord's brokers or the landlord himself. When my friend calls to complain, "Dallas, man, your guy is just being unreasonable," I can answer, "Dude, listen to me. These are the metrics that we've got to hit for our client. If we don't hit them, we won't be at your building. It's that simple."

To this day, one of the nicest compliments I've had a client give our firm is to tell some friends, "T. Dallas Smith & Company? They are pugilists! They will fight on your behalf. Period." It's great to get along with the folks on the other side of the deal. But at the end of the day, the assignment is always to get the best deals for our clients.

We don't pay the friendship tax. And most of the people with whom we interact already know that. They've seen us enough times now in the marketplace. At the end of the day, it's about math. And if the math is not what we need it to be, we've got to figure out a way to extract that. I've got a hell of a team—they are hella good. We have fun, but when it comes to protecting our clients' interests, we're all hardwired to do just that.

When we end up owning some buildings later on, I intend to make it a priority to ensure that interested clients know that from the start. Maybe they'll have to sign a conflict waiver, or better yet, I imagine we would encourage them to find other representation instead of us. To me, that's an important part of building and managing relationships. We're committed to playing one side of the table, and we're going to adhere to that because it's a very easy way to keep honest. It may be legal to play both sides, but I just think that makes it very difficult to be ethical. Something I say often to our potential clients is this: "Whether you hire us or not, pick a firm that represents your interests."

Far too many times, I've seen tenant clients willing to believe that the landlord's broker has their best interests at heart. And I can see how that happens with a broker who is good at endearing himself or herself to potential clients who don't have their own representation. "Here's my personal cell number. You call me anytime. I'm more than glad to help you." The whole narrative is "I'm here to help you," but what's left out is this: "I'm not representing you."

I always see a red flag whenever the tenant client I'm representing really likes the broker on the other side. That's the equivalent of drinking the Kool-Aid. I should know, because I was on the landlord's side my first six years in the business with Mr. Tift. I used to be the one making the Kool-Aid and serving it up. And now my whole job is to protect our tenant clients from helping themselves to a glass.

A situation similar to our experience at AT&T happened at FedEx much later on. With both companies, we were given little tests to see how we would perform. If we knocked those little tests out of the park, we'd earn something bigger, and on it would go from there.

It's not always clear how long it takes to build business relationships in a meaningful way. We didn't, for example, just land FedEx as a client out of the blue. Without Shannon Brown, FedEx would never have been possible. That story goes something like this: Back in high school, our chief operating officer, Dexter Warrior, had participated in the INROADS precollege program, a program that exposes talented students to corporate careers in computer science, technology, engineering, and business. Shannon had also participated in this program, and as successful adults—Shannon at FedEx and Dexter at T. Dallas Smith & Company—the two had been invited to serve on an INROADS panel together, where they hit it off. Dexter told Shannon, "You've got to meet my business partner, Dallas," and Shannon agreed.

The three of us initially met for lunch at Paschal's—one of H. J.'s restaurants. We had a ball together, laughing and talking about everything and anything. And we made that lunch meeting into a regular event.

About two years into our lunch meetings, Shannon offered, "I'm going to introduce you to the head of real estate for FedEx, Wiley Johnson."

Our experience with Wiley was much the same as with Shannon— we enjoyed one another's company, laughing and sharing stories. After having the opportunity to speak with his entire team, Wiley gave us four assignments—in Connecticut, Pennsylvania, Georgia, and Florida—to test out our abilities and to help us prove that a firm of our size and scope could do the work. We knocked each of those four assignments out of the park, and before long, we were working on FedEx projects up and down the East Coast, and heading out West, from New Jersey, to Florida, to Illinois, and to California.

As a firm, we're scrappy, and we're mobile, so we can maneuver a lot quicker than most of the bigger shops, which require all sorts of coordination. In a large brokerage, you've got to go through corporate to see if the guy in Houston can work on the deal in Georgia and whether the guy in Georgia can also help you in Los Angeles. Well, I've got twenty-two licenses myself, and among the lot of us at T. Dallas Smith & Company, I'm hoping we'll eventually be able to cover all fifty states when it comes to our ability to do business. In cases where we need coverage, we have partnerships with large commercial real estate firms with matching culture.

During the recession of 2006–2008, I'd regularly heard God telling me, "Enlarge your tent." At the time, I understood that directive as "Get licensed in multiple states." The world was coming apart, but I used that downtime to complete several continuing ed courses and earn state licenses—first regionally in the Southeast and then extending out from there. Those were the licenses that impressed Dexter when I invited him to our offices, and I'm engaged in the business of acquiring them; completing the continuing ed course for the state of Mississippi is my latest accomplishment. In a sense, by acquiring those licenses during that low point, I was laying out the infrastructure that would benefit the company I hadn't yet started. Nowadays, it's even more necessary to earn those credentials because technology, the great equalizer, has given us all access to the information we need within seconds of when we need it.

When I first got into the business in 1982, you had to situate yourself in a particular market or territory. I would get out the old-school Rand McNally maps and mark out the areas I planned to work. Then I'd knock on doors and find out who owned each building. Today I can learn all that in seconds from my phone. When you take geographic boundaries out of the mix, what you really need is a firm that's seen all types of deals and that can execute at the highest level. And that's where our firm comes into the picture. Between just Dexter and me—just two people—we've got eighty years in the business. And Dexter's a guy who did billions of dollars of transactions during his

Morgan Stanley days—all on the ownership side. When we bring our experience and our skills together on the tenant rep side, that's a hell of a lot of benefit to our clients.

Since Dexter came on board, it's been him, me, and Leonte leading the team, training up the group behind us to skillfully analyze our clients. We come on the scene like doctors meeting their new patients. "I hear you're having problems. Tell me what's going on." We do a careful and thorough evaluation, run the necessary tests, and then come up with the prescription to alleviate or resolve the issue.

Granted, it's taken time and a lot of intentional relationship building to get where we are today. Just because I had some relationships and Dexter had some relationships and Leonte was out there building still other relationships, those did not directly convert to getting business. I always tell people this: you've got to be able to balance patience and persistence with constant

> You've got to be able to balance patience and persistence with constant effort.

effort. That means checking in and circling back with potential clients just the right amount; letting them know you're there if they need something; and taking a genuine interest in their lives, their interests, their families. You do all that work steadily building relationships because people ultimately do business with people they like. If they like you and you can also do the work at the highest level, then you've found the winning combination.

I've hinted at it before, but I want to be clear about the level of effort we put in. Here's just one example: We'd gotten our first bit of business with a regional insurance company—this was one of those instances of a company testing out our abilities. They were downsizing from sixteen hundred square feet to nine hundred square feet. That was a deal any of us could do in our sleep. But all three of us—me, Dexter, and Leonte—drove a half day and across state lines to visit the existing space.

Together—and knowing full well that on-site managers can have a very different perception of needs than off-site company leadership—we met the managers there, face to face, and found out exactly what their pain points were. We saw firsthand what they needed, and understanding more thoroughly what they were trying to accomplish meant we could work faster on their behalf. We found them the right space, saved them some money, and turned the deal around quickly.

That's the kind of attentive effort we're putting into every deal. People refuse to believe me when I tell them the three of us went on a day trip for nine hundred square feet. A lot of the bigger shops, they're not going to get in the car and take a look at people's specific needs. They're just going to work from the plans on the paper. They're going to call the landlords and complete the entire deal without leaving their desks. But we do site visits for all our properties. I learned that from Herman J. Russell, who used to say, "You can't move real estate at the desk. You've got to go look at it."

That excellent advice has paid off more times than I can count. I remember traveling to Florida for an assignment that involved facilitating a dispossession for a big client. They wanted us to sell the property, but the values they assumed were much higher than what our research suggested. When I got to the site, I couldn't get in. There was a lockbox on the door, so I called the company's real estate office to ask, "Could you give me the code for the lockbox?" Turns out they had no clue there was a lockbox on the door. Eventually, the man heading up the office located a four-digit PIN from deep in his files.

What's the first thing I saw once I accessed the key and got into the building? A Toyota-sized hole in the roof.

I called the client to let him know what I was looking at, but he struggled to believe me. "Well, nobody has told us anything. There's nothing wrong with that building."

"All right. I'm going to send you a picture of what I'm looking at."

With him still on the line, I snapped a few photos of the palm trees swaying in the blue sky, visible through the Toyota-sized hole in the roof. That's what it took for him to believe me. "Let me call you back" was his only reply to seeing those photos.

It was that man's job to know the buildings in his portfolio, but who uncovered the issue? The guy who flew from Atlanta to Naples to go see the property for himself. We ended up selling the place for the price we anticipated, but that guy never even said thank you.

It's one thing to work with people who aren't appreciative of our efforts, but it's a whole 'nother thing to represent people who actively work against your success. What does that look like? Picture, for example, our company having been brought in by a client's CEO only to be treated disrespectfully by that client's middle management.

"And you are?"

"I'm Dallas with T. Dallas Smith & Company. We're here for the six seventy-eight Main and Second Street assignment."

I'm not the person they're used to dealing with. I'm not their golf buddy or good friend. I'll go out of my way to let them know they're in good hands, but often they'll actually put some effort into trying to cause a misstep for us so that they can say, "Well, we tried, and it didn't work out. Let's go back to our regular brokers."

Sometimes it's little things, like the time we noticed a water intrusion issue on a building and reported it to the property owner. "Oh yeah, we know about that; we know. We're handling it."

I remember sending a follow-up email to clarify: "Okay, glad to see you were already on top of the water intrusion issue at 123 Main Street. Just let me know if there's anything else that we can do for you." Fast-forward to three weeks later, and the water intrusion issue had moved an entire wall.

I received an irate call. "You guys are supposed to be taking care of this!"

Deep breath, and then: "Please refer back to my email on March twelfth where you stated that you were already on top of the issue and in touch with the third party who was handling it for you. I wrote back to you then, 'If there's anything else you want us to do, please let us know.'"

If we hadn't covered our asses in that instance, the whole situation would've turned on us in a heartbeat. That's how it is, unfortunately, and that's also why we are always trying to help our newest brokers understand that above all it's important to remember one thing: you're doing this work to help your client. Period. When you run across that one person who has got their feet dug in and communicates, whether by their words or their actions, "We've always done it this other way. Why are you here?" or "Why won't you go away?"—when that happens, you have to be ready to protect your client and your process.

There are other ways that clients push us away, some of them without even realizing that's what they're doing. I can't tell you how many times someone has asked us, "Are you sure you can do this all by yourselves?" I remember one client who, when we originally won their business, their point person refused to talk with anyone but the president and CEO of T. Dallas Smith & Company. About any deal. No matter the size.

It took a lot of time and effort to train that person away from wanting to deal only with me. I started by bringing Dexter in on the calls—Dexter, who has as many years in business as me. The first time I did that, this client double-checked, "Is Dallas there too?"

"Yeah, we're both here."

"Good, because I don't want to have to repeat myself."

It was like he was talking to four-year-olds.

Finally, over time, we wore him down, and he got used to talking to Dexter, then to Leonte, and then to some of our other brokers.

Still other clients will act like we're bothering them, putting them out. They'll answer the phone with "I've got a lot of stuff I'm working on. What is it that you need?" In many cases, we've been doing this so much longer than they have, and we know so much more than they do.

But here's the thing no one expects: we just keep doing what we know is right and exercising our patience. I sleep well at night because I know we take care of folks as if our lives depend on it. And the reality is that our lives do depend on it. I don't think it's mistaken to think of each deal like this: if we screw this one up, then my daughter's not going to school; or, if we screw this one up, then this will not continue to be our house. All we need is one client to say, "Whatever you do, don't hire T. Dallas Smith & Company." If a client says that, it's a wrap. We all know this adage: if you do something right, one person might find out about it, but if you do something wrong, at least ten people are going to find out about it. That commonplace confirms that everyone should try to do right by people all the time. That message is even more true when you're the underdog going up against the pack leaders.

That said, for all the ways in which I try and often succeed at getting along with most people, sometimes opportunities come our way, and we just have to say no. It might be a simple no, like when I received a call from a potential client on a Thursday afternoon letting me know that they were open to hiring us, but the proposal was due to them on Friday. I learned from *Seinfeld* that that's called an "unvitation." They don't want us to show up, but they want to be able to check the box saying, "Yeah, we invited them." The narrative on their side might be "Well, we reached out to Dallas, and he just wasn't interested."

Then there are slightly more complicated noes, as when we all traveled to an arranged meeting with a company's head of real estate, started telling our story, and got stopped midsentence with a "Hey, I don't need to hear all that."

I remember pausing in that moment, thinking, Okay, maybe, just maybe, he's about to say, "I don't need to hear all that. I already know about you guys. Let's figure out how to do some business together."

Instead he followed up with "I don't need to hear all that. I'm only here because our diversity and inclusion guy asked me to come."

"Well, okay. May I just ask you a question?"

"Sure."

"Who's handling your real estate right now?"

"One company handles all our stuff. They do everything we need."

"Let me just tell you this. Nobody's doing it like that anymore. Nobody. The largest firms, the ones that are really doing big things right now, they diversify everything. You've got all your eggs in one basket. That's never a good strategy for anybody. But hey, it's been great meeting you."

Dexter and I always remind ourselves that we're going to roll with the people who want to roll with us. I'm never going to try to twist somebody's arm or beg for their business. This work is hard enough on its own.

T. Dallas Smith & Company was just over four years old when my father died in 2010. He was able to see our new office space and was proud that we'd gotten AT&T and the federal government as clients. He saw the struggle, but he saw some of the wins too. Most importantly, he had a chance to meet the core guys—Leonte, who'd been with me from the start, and Dex, who'd just come on board.

I took a couple of weeks off work after my dad passed. On my first day back to work, I wanted to stop and grab some breakfast at the restaurant 40 Tables—a place I frequented given its nearness to the office and great food. Now, my dad's name was Willie Glenn Smith, and in the two-week period that I'd been away from the office, 40 Tables restaurant had changed to Glenn's Kitchen and started serving southern comfort food. My dad had been a hell of a cook. I didn't end up eating at Glenn's Kitchen that morning. I just looked at the menu and then decided to go straight to the office.

After settling in, I headed over to say something to Dexter, who looked up at me with the exact same soul-piercing "now is not the time" look that my dad used to give me.

"Okay, man. I can go. It can wait."

I tend to think that everything has a meaning, that even the most subtle or simple things can be packed with meaning, and that those meanings are important to whoever sees them.

I backed out of Dexter's space and for the first time thought about how much Dexter's temperament was identical to my father's. Without him saying anything, I could read exactly what he was telling me. Between that look from Dex and the arrival of Glenn's Kitchen, I felt like my father was telling me, "You're going to be fine. I got you. I'm covering you. And now you've got Dexter, and he has my proxy." I always tell people I was raised to work with Dexter. I know that we would cover each other, take a bullet for each other. That's much like how my dad was too. If you were a friend of his, you were good.

Dexter's mother always said to us, "The two of y'all fuss like brothers. Y'all fuss like brothers." We're two very strong type A guys; neither of us pull any punches. But I would submit to you that Dexter Warrior is also a very humble soul. On any given day, he could have decided to put up his own shingle and start his own successful firm. I'm forever grateful to him for choosing to work with me.

On the ten-year anniversary of our business partnership, one of my gifts to Dexter was a coin with his face on one side, mine on the other, and engraved with the saying "same coin, different sides." We were both raised by very good parents who loved us dearly. Our parents taught us the value of hard work, the value of treating people how we want to be treated, and the value of doing what you say you're going to do. That similarity in upbringing is part of our bond. Now, one of our differences is that Dexter is always looking for perfection and can build a monument to a little missed detail. If it's my tendency to go after the next big thing, it's his to drill down into it—to understand and maximize its benefit. To me, that balance between the two of us has been the secret sauce for our work.

The freaky thing is that Leonte is a perfect mix of us both. He's almost equal part Dexter, equal part Dallas, and part chameleon who is very comfortable in his own skin.

I've said before how absolutely critical it's been to have advocates and how much our company's business would not have moved forward without them. We're in a different place now than we were fifteen years ago because of the people—the Andy Ghertners, the Cort Bishops, the Wiley Johnsons, the Michael Fords, the Russ McFaddens, the Cherise Mlotts, and a host of others—who have lifted us up and given us opportunities, small and large, to prove our value.

That's why I'm so proud of the work that we do and the way that the three of us have built this business. We keep showing up without any heavy armor, just the commitment to our bond and to doing right by our clients. We persist, and every now and again, we land ourselves a Goliath.

My dad may have passed when T. Dallas Smith & Company was just getting its legs, but my mother saw a whole lot of what we'd accomplished before she died. She got to see us do some big deals, and she saw me get sworn in by the governor for the Board of Regents of the University System of Georgia. That event took place just a month before she passed. Contrary to her nature, she teared up at the swearing-in ceremony. My sister leaned in to ask her, "You good?" She was good, she said, just very proud.

CHAPTER 7

Mascot

My friend Egbert Perry is a brilliant guy who is also part of my brain trust—one of the people with whom I like to talk about ideas. In a recent conversation with Egbert, I found myself talking about "the three *m*'s." The way I see it, every successful entrepreneur goes through three distinct phases. The first thing you've got to do is Make it—turn your vision into an actual and sustainable reality. Then, once you make it, you've got to Manage it. That's about getting the right people in the right jobs, financing growth, and firmly establishing your business culture. Recently I've come to understand the third step as becoming the company Mascot. That's when people know the company because of you and think of it in terms of you. So, for example, Bill Gates hasn't been CEO of Microsoft for years, but people still relate Microsoft to Bill Gates.

I'm in the mascot phase now, where people associate my person with the brand that is T. Dallas Smith & Company. As a result of the mascot phase, a lot of opportunities have come our way. Potential clients and connections are reaching out to me like never before, and

125

I'm deep into thinking about how to make the mascot years really work for the company's growth.

Another of my friends calls this phase the celebrity phase, but I think the word *mascot* does a better job of conveying the kind of work that's still happening in this phase. If you've ever watched the mascot on the sidelines of a game, you know the mascot is doing a lot of grunt work, leaping into push-ups, doing backflips, and constantly responding to the crowd and encouraging their enthusiasm. Not all celebrity is like that.

As much as it can be exhausting work, being a mascot also garners a hell of a lot of attention. Two things are clear to me about this phase: First, everybody loves a winner when they're winning. That's to say, I'm very cognizant of another fate of winners, which is that people will destroy them if given the opportunity. Second, there's no room whatsoever in the mascot phase for the ego-driven guy that I was in my early twenties. I

The minute any one of us becomes ego driven, we're all in trouble.

think about how, as Schwartz's protégé, I moved around with the strongest sense that I was *that guy*. Now, knowing how dangerous that attitude can be, I'm well aware of the need to have guardrails—and guardian people—to keep that ego from inflating again. If that were to happen, we would no longer have a company. The line from scripture in Galatians 5:9, "A little leaven leavens the whole lump," sticks in my mind. The minute any one of us becomes ego driven, we're all in trouble.

The mascot has to be sensitive to the fact that any attention coming his way should be channeled toward the business in general—it's all for the sake of strengthening the company. If I do well in the mascot phase, there are so many benefits I can bring to our company and its people.

I can also bring that attention to important causes. Being a mascot requires thinking about having a platform and using it for good. In the fall of 2021, a year after doing the biggest real estate deal in the nation, I participated in a Sleep Out in conjunction with Covenant House Atlanta. That may have been the third year that I'd been involved with the organization—and the overnight fundraiser to provide shelter, stable housing, and employment for youth in the process of overcoming homelessness—but that was the first year that more than a handful of people acknowledged my participation. More than fifteen thousand people viewed my Instagram post from that night. A friend of mine offered an explanation for why I drew so much attention: "Dallas, sleeping out for homeless youth is the sort of thing people would expect someone else in your organization to do, not you." People are paying attention to what the mascot does—whether that's related to the business or to anything whatsoever.

Quite frankly, I'm befuddled by this phase. I'm still the kid who grew up off Simpson Road in Atlanta, Georgia, even though the attention currently coming my way would suggest otherwise.

Thankfully, within T. Dallas Smith & Company, we've established a culture that allows us to openly challenge one another, that keeps us each sharp and doesn't allow any one of us to get a big head. Scripture says, "Iron sharpens iron, and one man sharpens another" (Prov. 27:17). We've even set up our office suite to help facilitate that sharpening process. For the most part, it's a very open space. All the offices along the perimeter have glass walls, so there's a lot of visibility and access to whatever activity is going on. By design, there are no locks on our office doors; we invite one another into our spaces by simply removing any barriers to entry. There's only one opaque door in our entire suite, and that's the door to the conference room. That design detail was intentional; it's a reminder that if we're meeting in the conference room, we're meeting in confidence. Without question, if any of us are in that room, we're having a confidential discussion.

If you were to look into that conference room on any given day, you might think, These people are about to kill one another! You can see from our gestures that our voices are raised, can maybe even make out a comment or two through the glass. "Man, what the hell are you talking about?" "Man, that's just not so!" What we're fussing about is never personal. It's always an open disagreement about what's best for whichever client we're discussing.

If you've heard the story of the five blind men having their very first interaction with an elephant, you'll know what I'm talking about. Each one of us brings his specific knowledge and experience to the table, but each of us begins, in a certain sense, blind to the whole picture. When the blind men touch the elephant in different places, one comes away thinking he's touched a tree; another thinks it's a wall; a third thinks it's a water hose; and on they go recounting their differing experiences. In a sense, each of them is right to think as they do, but, of course, it's not until they put their descriptions and experiences all together—challenging one another's perceptions—that they get the best sense of the elephant as a whole.

A similar thing often holds true among our team members. I may believe we ought to do one thing, my business partner another, someone else yet another. Often we start off at a high pitch, each one believing in his plan and ready to support it with evidence. But what happens after a while—and sometimes a long while, with breaks, or occasionally the need to step away and sleep on a decision—is that we get to a far better answer collectively than any one of us had individually. Sometimes the way the pieces come together surprises us; we feel that "wow, look at what we've done here" pride in our work.

I realize I've imported that sharpening process from all my classes with Dr. Schwartz. He always expected us to support our positions in class and to seek and welcome feedback from the rest of the group. That process helped to ensure that none of us was the final arbiter of any decision.

I've seen other, more hierarchical, models in other companies, even amazingly successful companies. I remember working for Herman J. Russell and noticing that whatever he said became gospel. Of course, he and I would go at it on a regular basis. As much as I got on his nerves fussing about certain decisions, I always had the sense that he really appreciated the challenge. I remember a conversation where we were getting ready to go into a thirty-day close period on a piece of property. The contract was about to go hard in less than twenty-four hours; we were past our due diligence period and about to put money at risk. But H. J. hadn't done the due diligence work on this property.

I went into his office. "Mr. Russell, this contract's going hard in less than twenty-four hours, and you have not done any due diligence. You've got to do due diligence!"

He hit the table with his palm. "Darrell, before you were even born, I knew what was out there. Wasn't nothing out there but shotgun houses and rabbits. I'm not worried about it."

"Mr. Russell, with all due respect, you have no fucking idea what's in the ground. Anything could have happened since you grew up out there as a little boy. You don't live around there anymore. You don't know what's happened. And you won't know until you do your due diligence!"

He laughed. "You know, Darrell, you're right ... but I'm going to go ahead and do it my way. And if it comes back to bite me in the butt, I'm going to say, 'Darrell told me. He tried to get me right.'"

Mr. Russell died in 2014, and not long thereafter, T. Dallas Smith & Company represented his company when it moved its headquarters to Atlantic Station. Dexter and I were walking around the new space to have a look at the finished product, and we ended up being introduced to the company's general counsel, Yasmine Murray.

"You're Dallas Smith?" she asked, eyebrows raised.

"Yes."

"I need to talk to you."

"Am I ...? Oh, I think I'm in trouble," I joked.

I sat down in her office. "I'm going through all these contracts with Mr. Russell, and I see your name on a lot of them. Your name is on all these contracts for all this land over here."

"Yeah, I helped him buy a lot of land over there."

She paused and looked up at me. "Why didn't you ever do any due diligence?"

"Well, before I explain, could you please tell me what's happened?"

"There's a property off Stonewall Street. We started doing construction and found an old refrigerator in the ground. Then we found a Volkswagen Beetle in the ground!"

The way she told it, it sounded as if people had used the place as a dump for some time. So, of course, environmental remediation had to be done to clean it all up—all because H. J. hadn't done due diligence.

I told her the story of my conversation with Mr. Russell. "That makes all the sense in the world, Dallas." She laughed.

"The sad part about it is Mr. Russell's not even here for me to say, 'I told you so!'"

Can a company be successful with one decision maker at the helm? Yes, it can. But I've come to appreciate the value of collaboration and to see that not just good or wise ideas but the best ideas come from the full team's effort. At the end of the day, it doesn't matter who can lay claim to the outcome. What matters is that the client we're representing gets the maximum benefit from our collective brain trust.

There was a thirty-five-year difference between us, but in the thirty years I knew him, I could regularly be surprised by how much Mr. Tift and I had in common—our likes and dislikes, our motivations, and sometimes even our exact situations.

Back when I was twenty and he was fifty-five, we were both single men dating pretty women right around the time of the annual Atlanta Air Center Realty Christmas party for tenants and employees.

There was a big spread with turkey and ham, wine and beer, and we'd all gathered in midafternoon to kick off the celebration. After a bit, it became clear that the group was running out of alcohol. Before anyone could think to go to the store for more, Ray, one of the tenants, ran out to his car and brought back jars of moonshine he'd picked up on a recent trip to Alabama. We all transitioned from wine to moonshine with ease.

The company's party wrapped up around six o'clock in the evening. I was due to my girlfriend's house at six thirty so that I could accompany her to a Christmas party at her workplace at seven. Mr. Tift was also expected to report to his girlfriend's house to attend a holiday gathering with her.

I'd gotten drunk off the transition from wine to moonshine, so Tom Thompson and Kevin Lenz—themselves considerably less drunk than me—offered to take me over to my girlfriend's house. I got into the back seat and did my best to give them driving directions through my haze.

Picture two white guys pulling up to a Black apartment complex in an all-Black neighborhood with a very drunken Black man sitting in the back seat. Tom and Kevin helped me to my girlfriend Jackie's door, but the two of them stood in front of the door, whereas I stood off to the side. Tom knocked on the door. "Are you Jackie?" I heard him ask.

"Yes."

"We have a package we are deliverin' to you. We know you've got a hot date that you're goin' to tonight. Heeere's Dal-las!" Tom pulled me from the sidelines into the light. "All right, Dallas. You're good, all right, man? We'll see you."

Jackie was standing there giving me a "what in the hell" eyebrow raise.

"You ready to go, baaaby?" I offered.

No other words were exchanged for some time. We got into her car, and as she drove away from the apartment, she started having a whole conversation with herself. "I can't be-lieve this boy shows up like this! Drunk as a skunk. Hell no! Nuh-uh. This is not going to happen. You're not gonna meet my boss like this. You're not gonna meet my boss like this. Where is your car?"

"At the office."

"Hell no. Mnn-mmm. I cannot believe this."

Since I was in no condition to drive myself after Jackie dropped me off, I decided to go back into the office and wait there until I was sober enough to get home.

I used the entrance through Tift's office in the back of the building. There was enough ambient light in the room for me to see the silhouette of a man in front of me in the dark. I turned on the lights, and there was Tift sitting up on the table next to the tray of turkey.

"Tift, I thought you were goin' to a party!"

"I was goin' to the parrrty, but my girlfriend thought I was too drunk t'go to the parrrty!"

"Mr. Tift! My girlfren thought I was too drunk to go to the party!"

It was about eight o'clock. Mr. Tift and I sat there on the table with the turkey between us until we sobered up—around three in the morning. We just sat there and talked about everything under the sun—girls, real estate, politics. To this day, that's one of my favorite memories of him.

Mr. Tift died in the fall of 2021, as I was writing about my relationship with him in this book.

At the memorial service, I told a small group of mourners about talking with Tift into the night. As I'd remembered it, Tift and I both sobered up and went home before it was light out. Mr. Tift's assistant, Susan, remembered otherwise.

"Dallas!" she corrected me. "Y'all were both asleep when I got to the office the next morning! Tift was over on the couch, you were curled up on the love seat, and the turkey was just a carcass. You two had completely polished it off."

When Mr. Tift's family gathered for a smaller burial ceremony, I was the only Black man there. My mother had taught me to find out about people for myself, and my relationship with Mr. Tift had taught me the value of engaging with—rather than avoiding—people who appear as if they might not appreciate me. So when I saw that the people there were looking at me funny—and it's the same look no matter who's giving it—I took that as an indication that I should approach them rather than turn away.

I introduced myself, because I believe that if I have the opportunity, it's incumbent upon me to be present and initiate a conversation that helps to answer those unspoken questions—who are you? And why are you here?

I've known for most of my adult life that I've got to be overly conscious of how white people feel about me. But I've also known the possibility of changing others' hearts and minds—even the ones some might be inclined to think of as utterly set in their ways.

When I think about where I started from and how I got to where I am now—when I ask, How did I get here?—I am reminded of the value of treating other people the way I'd like to be treated. I'm not a special case, not an anomaly. I'm just intentional about relationships, and I think that a lot of the time, the mantra holds that you get what you put into them. Nothing in, nothing out. You've got to plant seeds—and then nurture them—to get a harvest. And just because you planted a seed today doesn't mean you'll see a harvest tomorrow. I have high standards when it comes to giving my honest answer to the question "Who have you met and what seeds have you sown today?"

> **You get what you put into them. Nothing in, nothing out. You've got to plant seeds—and then nurture them—to get a harvest.**

One of the pastors from my youth offered a lesson that I well understood at the time, having been a small boy who was teased and bullied about his nose: "You put a spell on people with your words." I thought about how my mother had very straightforwardly responded to my concern about being bullied by telling me that I had the nose of a king. Those few words changed everything for me, gave me the courage to stand up to my bully. But what if she'd said otherwise, if she'd said, "That's because you're not gonna amount to nothing, Ty"?

So I try to take care with my words and what they're casting out into the world.

It's my responsibility to do what I can to improve people's attitudes, maybe even change their minds. Not that long ago, I participated in a Diversity, Equity, and Inclusion panel at the C5 Summit in New York City—it was me; Mitch Rudin, CEO of Savills; and Allison Tomlinson, regional legal counsel at Gensler. One of the audience members, Bill from Naperville, Illinois, directed a question to me: "Well, you know, I hired a colored gal once." I could hear people shifting uncomfortably in their seats. "And my question is really how do I get them to assimilate to my culture?" This happened in the year 2021!

"So, Bill, I have a company where my business partner and I are the two oldest guys in the office, and everybody else is much younger than us. I don't have any hair, but I have got people on my team who have twists and locks and dreads and mohawks—all kinds of different hairstyles. And these are some of the brightest, smartest people you'll ever meet. And the reality is this, Bill: if I only hired guys that looked like me, thought like me, moved like me, our company would not move at all. So what I'd say to you, Bill, is that whenever you have the opportunity to bring people into your company who don't look like you, don't fit your mold, that's probably a good thing. You want them for that reason. You want them because they're going to bring something different to the table."

Bill paused for a moment.

"Hmm, that's a good way to think about it, Dallas."

I chose my words carefully because I needed Bill to hear me. If I'd started to talk about the racism embedded in his language, in his question, I imagined he'd be on the defensive. And what I wanted was to say something that might change his mind. I can't expect people to change who don't even know how what they're doing or saying might be offensive.

One of my mother's favorite lines from scripture, in her own words, was "Don't ever hide your light under a bushel; let your little light shine" (Matt. 5:15–16). When we were little kids, "This Little Light of Mine" was a song that we always sang in church. I'd sing that song so loud! I knew from Mom the importance of that light. "You've never hid in your life," she'd tell me. "And don't you ever start."

As an adult, I've thought about how much I'm hardwired to be a very social creature and very intentional about relationships. Part of that intentionality comes from attentiveness to how other people respond to me—the obvious responses as much as the very subtle ones, like changes in expression, position, demeanor. I'm hypersensitive to other people's emotions—both noticing them and even feeling them. When I see someone trip on the street and skin their knee, my response is visceral. My mother was very much like that. She was also very skilled at reading people. "No, that's not what she meant, Ty, that's not what she meant," she'd tell me about what someone had said during a conversation at the kitchen table. "She said that, but that's not what she meant …" Without question, my mom's assessments of what other people meant were spot on. I suppose I inherited some of that from her through some combination of genetics and the way she raised me. Today my experience of that gift, and the reason I think of it as a gift, is that it's not something I control in any way. Instead, I feel it. When I know what's going on with someone else, I just know.

I assume that explains why I get along with most people; I can read what they mean to communicate. I might attribute that ability to my mother, but I know full well that my dad was extremely proud of the fact that I could get along with so many different people. He had friends of every ilk—some might've been called rednecks and others might've been more like street guys, but they all had one thing in common. They loved my dad, and my dad was able to embrace each of them for who they were, wherever they were on their life paths. I'm proud of that part of me too—it's something about my dad that I've always wanted to emulate.

I often hear the comment from people, "Dallas, we just can't figure out how you do what you do!" But as I've said before, it's really very simple. I meet people looking to see what we might have in common. And I well know, too, that people want to be treated like people.

In the mascot phase of T. Dallas Smith & Company, I'm working on being even more careful that my words add rather than subtract from somebody else's life. That's always been true of the way I've tried to talk to the people I love—my wife, my kids, my closest friends. But now, as the company mascot, I see just how much people hang on to my words. If I say to a young broker, "Hey, man, let's go play golf together" or "Let's have lunch together," for me, I'm just playing golf or having lunch, but that person might approach me thinking, I'm having lunch with the CEO of the company.

Herman J. Russell may not have been big on giving compliments, but if he gave you one "attaboy," that was enough to make you feel like you could run through a wall. Granted, with Mr. Russell it may not have been an "attaboy" so much as a "you know, you ain't as dumb as you look, boy," but I remember how important it was for me to hear that from him, and how much it meant to my sense of myself and my own possibilities.

I understand that the mascot has a certain power, and I don't want to allow anybody to make me into a false idol. I was groomed by my parents to serve. And now the place I'm serving is in commercial real estate, bringing people who look like me into this space and finding our advocates. I realize the weight of people's words can be very heavy, and I try to be conscious of that and do whatever I can to use mine for good. If my gift is to be able to read people and build relationships with them, I want to be able to use that gift with surgical precision.

CHAPTER 8

Best Salesman I Ever Met

In the summer of my eighteenth year, I was living at home, trying to figure out who I was going to be and what I was going to do for work. I hadn't yet put my finger on commercial real estate as the career I wanted to pursue, but I had an inkling—and I'd been told by friends—that I'd be a good salesman.

Back then, if you wanted work, you read the want ads. I'd seen one that read "Sales manager training. No experience required. $$$$!" I was chasing money, so I picked up the phone and called the number. The guy who answered was enthusiastic. "Yeah, you got to come out. Come on out!"

The next day I went out to their site, a warehouse in the Smyrna area, near where the Atlanta Braves play now. There were a lot of other "sales manager trainees" there, about thirty of us. The guy from the phone call jogged out into the space, his enthusiasm jacked up even more than when we had talked the day before.

"Are you ready to make some money today? Are you ready to make some money today? If you can do what we're tasking you to do today, you'll never have to worry about money again in your life! I'm telling you! Never! We're going to pair you up with your sales trainers. Everyone go over there and pick a number."

My number was ten.

"Oh, Dallas, you got one of the best. You got one of the best!"

Then out came this other guy, my trainer for the day, wearing black slacks and a white shirt. He seemed old, but he was probably only ten or fifteen years my senior. "Are you ready to make some money today? Are you ready?"

"Yeah, okay! I'm ready to make some money today."

"Well, let's go get some money today!"

Our numbers corresponded to a series of closed curtains scattered all around the warehouse. Imagine a shower curtain hanging from tall ceiling tracks and closed in a tight circle around its contents. My trainer, Bobby, and I went over to shower curtain number ten. We opened it to see what we would be selling for the day.

Bobby pulled back the curtain. "Oh yeah. Oh yeah."

What he revealed was a pile of pots and pans. It was at this point that I started wondering, What the hell did I get myself into?

Bobby was encouraging. "Come on, come on. Get as much as you can!"

I grabbed as much as I could and followed him out to his car—one of those station wagons with wood paneling along its sides. He opened the trunk. "Man, go back and get everything you can." We made a couple of trips before the car was fully loaded.

It wasn't until we started our drive that Bobby revealed the next relevant bit of information: the number ten also corresponded to the area of town where we were expected to travel that day. Area ten was in Forsyth County.

Let me give you some perspective. Oprah Winfrey would later travel to Forsyth County to profile the area where, in the early 1980s, civil rights leaders had rocks thrown at them and were chased out by the Klan. In response to that act of terrorism, twenty thousand people marched on Forsyth County. My understanding of that incident reflected a fact I already well knew when Bobby and I started our drive that summer morning: there were no Blacks in Forsyth County.

But here were two Black men in a station wagon going to sell pots and pans there.

Bobby was in no way deterred. "Oh yeah. Oh man. You're going to love this! We're going to make some money today. We're going to make some money." The whole way there, he was full of excitement. "Oh yeah, we going to do this!"

After about twenty-five minutes, we came up on the town's main square. There was not a car in sight—just nobody around. I thought, Wooh, okay. Maybe we'll go downtown now instead.

Gently I asked Bobby, "Should we go somewhere else?"

"No, we got to figure this out." He drove slowly through the center of town. "Oh, here we go. Here we go. Here we go right here."

Bobby was pulling up on a church. Where there was a hearse. Because there was a funeral going on inside. Whoever had died was obviously a very important person in town, because the entire town appeared to be attending this funeral.

At that point, I was looking for a lifeline. Lord, you got to save me. Ain't no way in hell we're going to do this. We're going to be strung up. We're going to die out here.

I did a quick review: I'd graduated high school. I was living with my parents, no plan yet to go to college. And this was how my life was going to end.

"Man, come out here and grab a couple pots." Bobby was already heading toward the church, with me walking behind like a man on death row. Lord, please. Maybe there would be a lightning bolt or some other, quicker way I could leave the earth.

As we got closer, I could hear the music from inside, low and slow. Just in front of the door, there was a sign that read No Soliciting.

That sign was going to save us. "Bobby, we can't go in here."

"Dallas, some of my best clients have that same sign. Come on, man." Bobby swung the door open and marched inside.

I had my arms full of pots and pans; he had a pot in his hand. We turned a corner and immediately caught sight of two sheriffs. I'm talking good old boy, *In the Heat of the Night*, toothpicks-in-mouths sheriffs.

One of them came toward us. "Now I know you boys are not trying to sell pots and pans at a funeral."

I thought, I totally agree with you!

But it was Bobby who responded, "Sheriff, no, we are not trying to sell pots and pans. We are trying to save lives."

"Huh?"

"Sheriff, we …"

"Come on, fellas. Y'all got to get out of here."

The sheriff had put his hands firmly on both of our shoulders, moving us briskly toward the door. He was strong and had a big stomach on him, so Bobby offered, "Sheriff, now, you look like a man who likes to eat."

The sheriff laughed. "Yeah, my missus, she can really cook."

"Let me ask you something." Bobby took one of the pots from my arms. "Look at this." He flipped it over and back again. "Look at this. You think your missus would like something like this?"

"Yeah, she probably would."

"What you think something like this would cost?"

"Well, we bought something like that not too long ago. I think she paid one hundred fifty dollars, something like that."

Bobby leaned in. "I can do all of this right here for thirty dollars. Right now. Right now."

The sheriff shifted his toothpick, then put his hand in his pocket, took out his wallet, and gave Bobby thirty dollars. "All right, now, get on now."

"All right, man. We on our way, man. Thank you, Sheriff. Keep protecting us. Protect and serve."

I may have only been eighteen, but I learned a lot working with Bobby that day.

First of all, I had put up so many roadblocks to our success. I'd decided before we'd even started out that there was no way two Black guys headed to an all-white town were going to successfully sell any pots and pans—let alone make a sale to a sheriff guarding a funeral in a building with a No Soliciting sign out front.

That was not where Bobby's head was. Bobby knew we were going to make some money that day. And not just from that sheriff. By the end of the day, we'd sold everything we'd taken with us in his car.

My second lesson was an even more emotionally complicated one, because on that first day, I'd gotten intrigued by Bobby's uncanny ability.

"You'll be back tomorrow, right?"

"Yeah, I'll be back tomorrow."

The next day, our shower curtain revealed a pile of artwork, and our assigned territory was an office park in the Cumberland area. Artwork in our arms, Bobby led the sales pitch just as he had the day before.

"Hey, how you doing today? How you doing? This is a beautiful office. You know what you need? You need some beautiful paintings."

"Sir, you see the No Soliciting sign?"

"Hey, some of my best clients have that same sign. I want you to be another of my clients too."

Bobby went on from there, encouraging dialogue with the office assistant. That's when I saw Mr. Matthews, my homeroom teacher from senior year in high school.

"Ty? Tonialo? Tonialo Smith?"

I casually lifted the large painting I was carrying so that it covered my face up to my eyes. The way he said my name reverberated with disappointment, like "Oh God, Tonialo? This is what you're doing? Selling pictures door to door?"

I felt small, like a beggar.

And I didn't go back to the warehouse the next day.

It took me two days to learn that I didn't want to sell anything that wasn't directly helping people or making a clear improvement in someone's situation.

Bobby told the sheriff that he was saving lives—really he was hustling products that were near guaranteed not to have that effect. Quite frankly, if Bobby had been working in commercial real estate, he'd be a zillionaire right now. He was a master salesman. All Bobby needed was a genuine product to sell.

My dad always told a story about a very wealthy white man in his hometown of Newnan, Georgia. This man owed my granddad some money, and my father had been sent to retrieve it. So the man picked up a paper bag, tore off a scrap, wrote "Pay Willie $5," and added his signature. He handed the slip of paper to my father with the instructions "Take this piece of paper down to the bank. They'll give you the five dollars." That's exactly what my dad did, and the man's debt to my grandfather was paid.

For me, what stands out about that story is not so much the point that no such gesture could have the same effect in today's world. Instead, what stands out to me is that when a person signed his name, that meant something. I think about all the businesses that were named for their founders—Heinz, Johnson & Johnson, H. J. Russell. Putting one's name on something meant putting one's reputation on the line. That name was a promise: I guarantee that this is a quality product. And if something goes wrong, you've got one throat to choke. You call me. It's my job to go find out what the problem is and to fix it.

I grew up in an era when if you stood behind a product, you purposefully put your name on it. That's why T. Dallas Smith & Company is named after me. My name carries the bond of my word. I remember early on, just after Dexter had come on board, we were at an industry gathering, and one of our business colleagues was arguing with Dexter. "You've got to change the name of the company."

I remember hearing Dexter say, "No. We're good."

"No, no, seriously."

"No, really, we're good."

Dexter knew why the company was named after me, and he was good with that. It wasn't a matter of anyone's ego. It was, and is, about guaranteeing a product.

We talk about entrepreneurs and founders like they're doing the exact same work, but I like to distinguish the two. If you're an entrepreneur, you're likely doing something that's already been done—like owning a business franchise. If you're a founder, there's an additional level of risk because you're doing something that hasn't quite been done before, or that someone else tried but never succeeded at. And you're putting yourself on the line in every step of the risk-taking.

That's one of the reasons I believe that being a founder requires a sense of calling or faith that one's efforts will succeed. I also believe that founding something—especially in the service professions—requires a singular focus. When I was getting the business up and running, I remember people asking, "Well, if this doesn't work out, Dallas, what will you do?"

"Well, it's going to work."

"But how do you know it's going to work?"

"I can't tell you how I know it's going to work. I just know it's going to work. I know I'm doing what I'm supposed to do."

When I started the company, I had no plan B and no thought of needing a plan B. I thought about it like this: God told Noah to build an ark. But what if Noah had said, "Yeah, okay. But just in case I'm not able to build that ark, how about we try floating some palm fiber baskets and see what we can save that way?" That's not how faith works. Having a plan B is similar to walking on a high-up tightrope with a net beneath you. Without the net, you've got to be extraordinarily focused on the wire. If you've got a net, just glancing at the net could be enough to take away your focus and cause you to fall. Falling into the net might mean that plan A never worked because you never really focused on plan A like you should have.

> Falling into the net might mean that plan A never worked because you never really focused on plan A like you should have.

My focus was on tenant representation—office, industrial, land—and that was singularly our lane. The idea of it not working never entered my mind. And it's remained true for me: not losing faith or growing weary even in my well-doing but staying focused on the wire. There is scripture from Proverbs 22:29 that says, "Do you see a man who excels in his work? He will stand before kings." I've always made sense of that by thinking about how the king wants the best. If you cut grass unlike anybody else, the king wants you to cut his grass. If you develop your gifts, those gifts will eventually make room for you.

I've always thought I had a gift for selling, but I've never thought about that gift as merely transactional, merely a hustle. Instead, for me—at least after I met Bobby and learned something about my own motivations—selling has been about intentionally building relationships. The sales transaction, if and when it happens, is just one piece of that relationship. Mind you, it's no small piece when you put your word and your name behind your product. But it's really only a part of something much bigger.

Back when we first got one of our biggest clients, we divided work assignments among a small group of us at the office. The only task one of the brokers had was getting in contact with the current landlord and letting them know that we were the new firm representing the client on this assignment.

At our weekly meeting, I asked, "Have you talked to the landlord?"

"No, haven't gotten ahold of him."

"Okay, let me know when you do."

The same exchange happened the next week. "Haven't got ahold of him."

Two whole months went by. I couldn't figure out what was holding things up. "Okay. So help me understand. When you call him, what is he saying to you?"

"Oh. No, I haven't called him. I've been sending emails."

"You've got to understand. People my age, in a transaction like this—you're not going to get ahold of them sending emails. Do you have the number?"

"Yes."

I dialed.

"Dallas, hey! I've been waiting to hear from you."

"Yeah, we're trying to get this renewal done. Here's the rate … and here's what we need to do …"

"Done and done."

I hung up and handed this broker one of the erasable markers from my desk. "Please write this on the window over there: 'You can't build meaningful relationships via email, texts, or tweets.'"

There's one other statement written on the window just beneath that one. It was written after I'd asked another young broker what was going on with one of our contacts.

He said, "Dallas, I don't really think they will be a help, so I haven't followed up."

"What?"

"The position that they're in, I don't really think they can help us with this."

"Man, it's not about chasing a transaction. It's about building relationships before you need them. You find me anybody who's been with a company more than ten years and getting good reviews—I don't care what position they're in. They're going to know some important people."

You'll remember my friend James Arnold, the shoeshine man who worked in the building where our Cushman & Wakefield offices were located. James was the relationship guy. When Steve Jobs was trying to get a meeting with Dr. Thomas Mensah—the man who created Cat 5 wiring—nobody knew how to get ahold of Mensah until they called my friend James and told him what they were trying to do. A couple of days later, James had arranged a meeting between Jobs and Mensah at the shoeshine stand. That would never have happened if the people involved were thinking about job titles as signs of other people's importance or value. The world is very small. You never know who you'll need or who will need you.

> **The world is very small. You never know who you'll need or who will need you.**

"You never know who knows who," I cautioned the young broker. "Take this marker and write on the window 'Build relationships before you need them.'"

When I recommend building relationships before you need them, I mean over the course of a lifetime.

For a recent holiday, my team and I were scheduled to wrap gifts for the Families First organization. Everyone was supposed to be there at twelve thirty, but I saw that our admin had put the event on my calendar for noon. I checked in with my assistant.

"Ms. D, why am I going thirty minutes earlier than everyone else? Have they got me wrapping extra gifts or something?"

"Well, they called and said the CEO wanted to meet with you first."

It wasn't until I got there that I looked again at my calendar to see who I was meeting with. That's when I saw the name: DePriest Waddy. It sounded so familiar, but I couldn't quite place him.

Before I even got to the receptionist's station, DePriest was there to greet me and invite me into his office. That's when the connection became clearer to me. "Can I ask you a question?"

"Sure."

"This is going to sound strange. Do you have a daughter?"

"Yeah. I have a daughter."

"What's your daughter's name?"

"Jordan."

"My mother used to keep your daughter!"

"Your mother loved kids."

I was probably about twenty-six years old and working at Cushman & Wakefield when my mother kept Jordan for day care. I had hair then and was thinner, and, of course, everyone called me Ty.

It turns out the reason DePriest wanted me there early was to ask if I'd be willing to receive a community impact award at their annual banquet. I got emotional when I agreed to it.

Just imagine if I had treated this guy poorly or somehow less than back when I was a twenty-six-year-old. Or imagine if Herman J. Russell had decided not to talk with me when I cold called him from Cushman & Wakefield. He didn't know me from Adam, but he called me back in fifteen minutes. I remember his explanation: "I didn't know why you called me, Dallas. I would only know why you called me if I called you back. Maybe you needed some help from me. Maybe you had a job for me. I just wouldn't know until I called you back."

That's relationship building. When he picked up the phone, he didn't know that later on I would run a brokerage division for him and help him assemble a whole city block in Atlanta. He didn't know that I'd be one of his pallbearers when he passed. You can't know any of that kind of thing ahead of time. What comes out of a relationship will come out of the relationship—whatever that is. You invest in people before you know anything about where you or they are headed.

When DePriest introduced me to his COO, he said something that meant the world to me: "If you knew Dallas's parents, you would understand why he is so successful." My mom and dad were the kind of people who would give others the shirts off their backs. My mother always said that God had been good to her family, and she was always going to return the favor if she could. Money comes and goes, but how you treat people—how you make people feel whenever you're in their presence—can last a lifetime.

DePriest added, "Oh, and the barbecue! Your dad made the best barbecue, hands down. Ribs were almost purple."

He's been dead for some time now, but people still talk about my dad's ribs. I think that's as good as any example of what it means to build relationships. You don't go into them because you need something. You go into them to meet people, to make friends, to treat people like people, to enjoy your time together. If friends find ways to help each other out, that's a different thing from a simple transactional encounter.

One of my dear friends, Jerry Jones, gave me some of the best help I've ever received right after I'd gotten divorced from my first wife. I was in my early thirties, and I'd moved back home with my parents for some time. I was stressed out and depressed, and I explained to Jerry that I needed to be sure to make all my child support payments absolutely on time—even ahead of time if I could.

Jerry offered a potential solution to my problem. "Man, I want you to come with me to the flea market."

"What are you talking about?"

"Man, just come to the flea market. You can sell your stuff and make some money."

"Jerry, I don't have anything to sell."

"I don't care what you got. Whatever you've got that you want to throw away, just pack it up and bring it to the flea market. The only thing you can't sell is underwear. But just damn near everything else you can sell. Man, you got old shoes, clothes …"

He came by the house to help me pick out what to bring.

"What's that?" Jerry asked.

My parents had these boxes of Sharpies and other markers that had been in the garage for years; I'm talking maybe five hundred markers. The dust on those boxes was an inch thick.

"Bring that."

I paid ten dollars to set up a card table for all my stuff. We weren't there ten minutes before this woman came up to the table. "Are those markers?" The markers sold for $200. After the markers, I sold every pair of shoes I'd brought for five dollars a pair. Everything I brought with me that day got sold.

Jerry has always been a dear friend, always supportive whether I've had money or not, been happy or not. It was Jerry who was my comedy partner for the Pedro and Wallace routine—making up wild stories, making people laugh, and finding a way to make a little money enjoying ourselves.

You know the adage: It doesn't take anything to have friends when you've got a million dollars. But when you have absolutely nothing and you see those few people still standing there with you? Those are your friends. Jerry. Cousin Eric ... those are guys who've been with me through thick and thin. Those are people who understand the power of relationships.

In recent years, I've learned an important lesson about building and sustaining relationships.

I've dedicated the past fifteen years to building a company with an explicit commitment to making sure that we create an environment that gives everyone an opportunity. But I've come to see that no matter how admirable the sentiment or my own sense of my skill as a relationship builder, achieving that goal has required that we change some things about how the company functions. I'd noticed that as we'd grown the business, we'd had no trouble hiring Black women brokers. But we did struggle to retain them.

As a Black man who got his start in an office full of white men, it was rough to discover that I'd inadvertently created a parallel good old boys' shop, a bunch of Black men getting on in ways that made Black women feel excluded. In our conversations about how to improve the company's capacity to retain Black women brokers, Dexter and I talked about the need to bring on board a well-established Black woman broker as part of company leadership. The person we hoped we could invite to join us was Audra Cunningham.

Audra Cunningham transitioned into corporate real estate back in 2008 after being a telecommunications executive for much of her career. A lot of firms initially resisted her attempts to pivot into this business. Then a man named Steve Dils with a company called Grubb & Ellis hired her and gave her a chance. She eventually moved from there to several big commercial real estate firms and made a name for herself along the way. We knew she would be a hell of a person for us to bring on board, and we talked with her about making sure to let us know when she was ready to make her next move.

Audra has been our chief administrative officer for the past couple of years now, and what's been wonderful about having her on the senior executive team is that she's driven to fulfill the same mission that guides us—to expose to the industry people who look like us. She's laser focused on ensuring that Black women can become in all ways equal in this industry. And I'm thankful to her for helping us continue to grow our capacity for building strong relationships by strengthening representation on this team.

CONCLUSION

I was standing in a 7-Eleven one morning in a long line of people at the checkout. The cashier was on her phone having a full—and fully audible—conversation with a girlfriend.

After a bit, I stepped out of the line. "Ma'am. Let me just tell you something."

Everyone grew silent, including—to everyone's surprise—the cashier. "Ma'am, this job is not for you. This is not what you want to do."

"Girl, let me get off this phone. I got this guy here." She turned to look me in the eyes. "What did you say?"

"This is not for you. This is not what you want to do. All these people here, we're standing here and listening to you on that damn call. We're just trying to buy chips or gas and get out of here. This is obviously not meant for you. Please go find something that's meant for you, because this is not it."

The people in the line started clapping.

I can't say that those people were clapping for the point I was trying to make. But I can say that I meant it. I want people to wake up in the morning and want to go do work that feels right for them. I don't think it's naive to hold this belief. If there's something you enjoy doing and you want to get paid to do it, then your destiny is tied to that thing. And if there's any chance at all for you to do that thing, go do it; one day you may be paid well for your effort. That means you'll need to think of any jobs you had to take along the way—all the ones you didn't, and don't, want—as temporary stepping stones along a path that gets you from here to there.

Those jobs don't have to be your lot in life. Wherever you are right now doesn't have to be your final destination. And one good way to get out of your own way is to take a careful look at what you enjoy doing. This 7-Eleven cashier was present at a job at the expense of doing her job. What might happen if she were to put all her energy and focus into something she enjoyed?

As T. Dallas Smith & Company has received more recognition in recent years, I've regularly had to review my reasons for starting it. That's not just the story of Leonte's patience in the early days as he waited for me to teach him the business or his generosity in believing that I would eventually do just that. Instead, my reasons go back to the very basics. When God told me to build this business, I understood my calling very clearly: Work on exposure. Bring more Black people into this industry. Even today, as I write this, Black people still make up only about 3 percent of this industry's workforce. In other words, there is still quite a lot of work to be done.

I find myself saying the same things today that I said when I started out:

1. Exposure is everything.

It's hard to aspire to anything you've never been exposed to. Leonte started out looking to me as his model, someone who'd accomplished the same things he hoped to accomplish. Today, as an industry, we might have some mentorship programs in place, but we still have a way to go when it comes to welcoming more Black people—and particularly Black women—into this field.

2. People can change.

Mr. Tift was the son of a Klansman who eventually referred to me as his son. My mother's lesson to me—that I should see for myself about people—and my father's example—that meaningful friendships could be developed across seemingly insurmountable boundaries—have been the top influences on my own capacity to build lasting relationships with people who some might think hold incorrigible views.

3. Opportunity is essential.

Someone has to open the door. For us, it's very simple: like Uncle Sam, we want you! I'm also extremely proud that many brokers who get their start at T. Dallas Smith & Company are able to go off to opportunities at other shops that may not have been offered to them otherwise. I am proud to have provided that opportunity.

4. Know who truly supports and believes in you.

My mother told me I had the nose of a king. My father showed me how to make friends of everyone I met. Dr. Schwartz thought I was *that guy*. My true friends stick with me through the high highs and the low lows. They believe in me against all doubters, and their support is invaluable.

5. Develop a healthy ego.

I learned firsthand the risks of having too big an ego. I know that it's important to balance wanting to be seen and acknowledged with ensuring that you become someone who sees and acknowledges other people.

6. Always look for solutions.

My billionaire friends have a finger on something important. No matter what they're facing, they have the ability—and the resources—to look for solutions. I don't believe that mindset is reserved only for billionaires. I'll never forget that when I was broke, owed money, and was living with my parents, Jerry helped me find a reasonable and immediate solution to a problem I was facing. Considering all the options when you're problem solving can be a big factor in reaching toward success.

7. Walk before you run.

Herman J. Russell shined shoes and sold bottles of cola long before he owned a multimillion-dollar corporation. Wanting to sprint is a great aspiration. But please don't forget that before sprinting, there's crawling, stumbling, falling, walking, eventually running … It's taken me a lifetime to build the foundation on which I know my successors will continue to build. I'm proud of having been able to lay that foundation, but I also know there's a long way yet to go.

8. Look for your Branch Rickeys.

Everyone needs advocates, and Black people working in commercial real estate still need every white advocate they can get. Vet those people carefully, but also believe them when they show you who they are the very first time and what they're willing to do for your benefit.

9. Authenticity is the only currency that really matters.

I treat people how I want to be treated, period. And I go out of my way to hold off on forming an opinion until I meet people and get to know them. I also keep front of mind that I may be the very person who, by being 100 percent myself, helps to change someone else's opinions or ideas, or even someone else's heart. Remember the possibility that you may be the person who changes someone else for the better.

10. Know your gifts.

And use them for good. I was lucky to have had a mother who helped me identify my people-reading skills and hone them. But I've met too many people who haven't even considered what their unique gifts and tools might be. Find out from other people what they see in you and find ways to develop those abilities and talents to benefit others.

11. Build relationships before you need them.

I mentioned early on the value of really meeting people when you're introduced to them—the value of finding out something more than surface details and sharing enough of yourself to see what you and someone else might hold in common. I've been floored by the surprising ways I've felt connected to people who started off as strangers to me. I've also been happy to experience the give-and-take that comes from a place of trust; I know that trust is the product of being truly present for others and expecting the same in return.

You'll recall that Brian Jordan introduced me to Leonte at my lowest point; Brian and I had had our best-laid plans ruined by the housing market bubble. Looking back on it now, I'm grateful to have gone through the experience of losing everything at that point because I might not otherwise have met Leonte, and I very likely would not have felt the calling to invite Leonte to join me in starting the company that I intend to make him president of on my sixtieth birthday in 2022.

It was Leonte who thought big from the very beginning, who had a vision for turning our little operation into a billion-dollar company that would contribute directly to boosting diversity within the industry. I remember listening to his ideas and thinking, Okay, sure, sure. Let's see what happens—never for a second imagining that, fifteen years later, we'd do the biggest deal in the United States and find ourselves in a position to map out the big moves he'd envisioned.

When I first hired Leonte, he was a college sophomore—just as I was when Mr. Tift hired me. Once I had my epiphany about starting T. Dallas Smith & Company, my plan was always to prepare Leonte to take over the company. Here was this kid I had tried my best to get rid of doing every little thing I asked him to do with a heart of service and a warm smile. When I finally took Leonte under my wing, I well knew that this would be the man who would run the company. "Train him up as a son," God had said. "Give him everything; share the good, the bad, and the ugly."

That's been remarkably easy to do. Leonte is wise beyond his years, an old man in a young man's body, with just the energy the company needs moving forward. I believe that Dexter and I have laid a good foundation and that Leonte has the vision to carry the company into the coming decades.

When I think about the future of T. Dallas Smith & Company, I'm reminded of Schwartz's big lessons, none more than this insight memorialized in *The Magic of Thinking Big*: "Think 'I can do better.' The best is not unattainable. There is room for doing everything better. Nothing in this world is being done as well as it could be."[1] I've been in this business for forty years, but in some ways, T. Dallas Smith & Company is just getting started, and it can always do better.

We have our foundation and a clear story of how we got to where we are today. If I've told it well, I'll have convinced you that there is already a lineage of Black commercial real estate success stories into which many others will one day fit. I'll have convinced you, too, of the work we've yet to do ensuring that Black men and women are informed about the commercial real estate industry, empowered to find their way in it, and eventually authorized to change the narrative for good.

---

1   David J. Schwartz, *The Magic of Thinking Big* (Touchstone, 1987).